OTHER TITLES IN OTTO PENZLER'S
SHERLOCK HOLMES LIBRARY

BAKER STREET STUDIES

H. W. BELL

OTTO PENZLER BOOKS
New York

**Otto
Penzler
Books**

Otto Penzler Books
129 West 56th Street
New York, NY 10019
(Editorial Offices only)

Simon & Schuster Inc.
Rockefeller Center
1230 Avenue of the Americas
New York, NY 10020

Manufactured in the United States of America

1   3   5   7   9   10   8   6   4   2

Library of Congress-in-Publication Data
Baker Street Studies/edited by H. W. Bell
p.   cm.
Originally published: London: Constable, 1934.
1. Doyle, Arthur Conan, Sir, 1859–1930—Characters—
Sherlock Holmes. 2. Detective and mystery stories, English—
History and criticism. 3. Holmes, Sherlock (Fictitious character)
4. Private investigators in literature. I. Bell, H. W. (Harold Wilmerding)
PR4624.B284   1995
823'.8—dc20   94-22580   CIP

ISBN 1-883402-91-3

CONTENTS

v

INTRODUCTORY NOTE

L'homme n'est rien, l'œuvre tout ![1] To this
sentiment in one of Flaubert's letters to George
Sand Holmes lent the weight of his approval;
and as we all know, on several occasions he
reproached his biographer for injecting an
element of romance into what, in his opinion,
should have been a serious scientific study. He
would have preferred to have his cases recorded
as coldly and impersonally as a problem in
Euclid, with no more irrelevant material than is
found in Flaubert's own adored Spinoza.

But not even the most docile and devoted
companion of a great man can wholly put off his
own nature at another's behest and take on a
different habit of mind; if he is an artist the feat
becomes quite impossible. Rather than change
his attitude towards his art, Watson suffered his
friend's unfriendly comments in silence, not
concerned to justify himself. For he had the true
artist's inward assurance that he was right, deeply

[1] By some deplorable accident, the printer of the *Strand*
altered this to *L'homme c'est rien—l'œuvre c'est tout*. The
error has persisted in all subsequent editions.

vii

aware that, as George Sand insisted to Flaubert in her reply, *La suprême impartialité est une chose antihumaine . . . la qualité essentielle lui manque: l'intérêt.*

This one essential Watson made it his life's work to seize and note down. His reward is a Sherlock Holmes who is not a fading memory at Scotland Yard, nor a bloodless ghost lurking in library basements where the newspaper-files are stored away, but a Holmes who dwells for ever with the blessed immortals, in a state transcending the limitations of space and time.

But when a mortal has thus put on immortality, his devotees make haste to scrutinise his acts, his words, and his very thoughts, as under a microscope, in order to forestall the attentions of the Devil's Advocate. They themselves are at pains to be the first to call attention to seeming flaws in their hero, and in the next breath to show how these difficulties may all be easily reconciled, to the confusion of the impious.

And thus it is that we, who have survived or who have not known the epic age of the Victorian heroes, are following in the footsteps of the Alexandrian scholars and have become glossators, commentators. To a glossator every detail is precious. He is as eager to verify an uncertain date as to determine the conditions of the hero's early life and training ; he feels it imperative to define his ambiguous attitude towards the opposite sex ; and, though with shuddering and awe, to contemplate his human limitations. His brother, though infrequently mentioned in the sources, will be an object of study ; and if he, how much more the faithful biographer upon whose piety the glossator is wholly dependent. His great opponent cannot escape minute investigation ; and even the humble and self-effacing landlady is assigned her niche in the gallery of the hero's fame.

Such, then, has been our task. The studies here presented are in the nature of surface-finds ; but the lode runs deep and contains inexhaustible ore. It is for you, our readers, generous and enthusiastic (if such you are indeed) to signify in the only intelligible manner if we are to excavate this hidden wealth, and offer it for your enrichment and delight.

H. W. BELL

EXPLANATION

IN the notes, references to the Stories are to the two-volume edition published by John Murray.[1] This, the first collected edition, the only one corrected by the Author, must be regarded as definitive.

For convenience and brevity, the roman numeral I is used to indicate the volume of Short Stories, and II that of the Long Stories. The titles of the adventures referred to are likewise given, unless clearly indicated in the text.

[1] *Sherlock Holmes...The Complete Short Stories* [1928]; *Sherlock Holmes...The Complete Long Stories* [1929].

Holmes' College Career

DOROTHY L. SAYERS

' *Is there any other point to which you would wish to draw my attention ?* '

' *To the curious incident of the dog.* '

SILVER BLAZE

BAKER-STREET STUDIES

I. HOLMES' COLLEGE CAREER

THE evidence as to Holmes' college career rests upon two short passages, occurring in the adventures of The ' Gloria Scott' and The Musgrave Ritual respectively. Brief as they are, these passages contain more than one apparent contradiction, and present a curious and interesting series of problems to the critic.

The passage in The ' Gloria Scott' is as follows:—

' [Victor Trevor] was the only friend I made during the two years that I was at college. I was never a very sociable fellow, Watson, always rather fond of moping in my rooms and working out my own little methods of thought, so that I never mixed much with the men of my year. Bar fencing and boxing I had few athletic tastes, and then my line of study was quite distinct from that of the other fellows, so that we had no points of contact at all. Trevor was the only man I knew, and that only through the accident of his bull-terrier freezing on to my ankle one morning as I went down to chapel.' [1]

The passage in The Musgrave Ritual also purports to be Holmes' *ipse dixit*. It runs :—

' When I first came up to London I had rooms in Montague Street . . . and there I waited, filling in my

[1] I, 375.

3

too abundant leisure time by studying all those branches of science which might make me more efficient. Now and again cases came in my way, principally through the introduction of old fellow-students, for during my last years at the university there was a good deal of talk there about myself and my methods. The third of these cases [1] was that of the Musgrave Ritual. . . . Reginald Musgrave had been in the same college as myself, and I had some slight acquaintance with him. . . . In appearance he was a man of an exceedingly aristocratic type. . . . He was indeed a scion of one of the very oldest families in the kingdom. . . . Now and again we drifted into talk, and I can remember that more than once he expressed a keen interest in my methods. . . . For four years I had seen nothing of him, until one morning he walked into my room in Montague Street.' [2]

Tantalisingly meagre though they are, these two passages are of the utmost importance, since they are almost all that we have to go upon in establishing, not merely the educative and formative influences which presided over our greatest detective's youth, but also the actual date of his birth. It will, therefore, not be wasted labour if we examine them with particular attention, in the hope of answering these questions, viz. :—

[1] It is not clear whether Holmes means actually ' my third case' or, more specifically, ' the third case obtained by means of these introductions.' The former interpretation has found greater favour with the critics, but the latter is at least possible, and offers more elbow-room to the student of Holmes' chronology. See below, p. 9.

[2] I, pp. 399 ff.

(A) Which was Holmes' university?
(B) How long did his academic career last?
(C) When did he matriculate?
(D) In what year was he born?
(E) What subject or subjects did he study?
(F) Which was his college?
(G) What did he do immediately after leaving college?

Much of the vagueness which has attended the efforts of previous commentators to handle the matter has arisen from the assumption that the regulations governing the older Universities were the same in the 'seventies as they are to-day. It is taken for granted that the Final Examinations were held in the Easter Term, and that an undergraduate would, in the ordinary course of events, always come into residence in October and go down in June. It will be seen that this was not by any means the case. The whole question is considerably more complex, and the alternatives that present themselves are so numerous as to make any precise conclusion difficult in the extreme. I shall hope, in the following pages, to determine the conditions of the problem with a little more precision than has been attempted hitherto, and to put forward some sort of tentative answer to all the queries in my list.

(A) Considering first that simple dichotomy

which forms so complete and satisfying a disjunction of the academic universe, we have to ask ourselves : Was Holmes at (*a*) Oxford or Cambridge, or (*b*) one of the others ? Here, at least, we can speak with some measure of certainty. There is no doubt whatever that he passed a portion at any rate of his time at one of the older universities. It is not for one moment conceivable that Reginald Musgrave (whom Holmes could never even look at without associating him with grey archways and mullioned windows) could, in the 'seventies, have been connected with any provincial place of learning. On this point most commentators are agreed.

Blakeney, however, in his stimulating little work, *Sherlock Holmes : Fact or Fiction ?* makes the interesting suggestion that, after only two years at Cambridge, Holmes ' preferred to gravitate to London,' which thus ' has claims to Holmes's student days.' [1] He bases this suggestion on the following data :—(1) That Holmes specifically speaks of ' the two years that [he] was at college,' [2] (2) that at the time of the *Gloria Scott* case he already had rooms in town, (3) that during the (Cambridge) long vacation he was doing chemical research in London, (4) that as

---

[1] T. S. Blakeney : *Sherlock Holmes*, pp. 5, 4.
[2] *The ' Gloria Scott*,' loc. cit.

late as 1881 he was utilising the laboratories at Bart's, (5) that London was better suited to his ' desultory studies ' than one of the older universities, and (6) that Holmes speaks of ' coming up ' to London at some time before the affair of *The Musgrave Ritual*.

This theory, persuasive as it seems at first sight, will not, I think, hold water. Let us take Blakeney's points in order. Point (1) raises at once the great question of the discrepancy between Holmes' own two statements, namely, that whereas in the *Gloria Scott* account he declares that he was only two years at college, in the *Musgrave Ritual* account he speaks of his ' last years ' at the university. Blakeney's theory is apparently designed to reconcile these two conflicting statements, but, as we shall see, it does not do this and, in failing to do so, loses much of its reason for existence. Point (2) implies that Holmes' affiliation to London University began in the October of the same year that saw the adventure of *The ' Gloria Scott '* (for if it does not mean this, it has no bearing on the matter). We shall find that to assume this involves us in some serious chronological difficulties. For the moment, however, it is enough to say that there is nothing to prevent a Cambridge undergraduate from taking rooms in London in order to pursue

7

a course of reading in the long vacation, and that Holmes' narrative implies, on the whole, that at the end of his vacation he intended to return to the university from which he had come. This observation contains in itself the reply to Point (3). Point (4) seems to have little bearing on the question, since permission to use the laboratories could be obtained by a qualified research student from another university. Point (5) has some force, and it is by no means impossible that Holmes undertook some kind of postgraduate course in London in 1876 or 1877, but not (I think) at the early date which Blakeney suggests. Point (6) contains in itself its own best refutation. Blakeney admits that Holmes ' came up ' to London ' seemingly after leaving the 'Varsity ' and ' settled down to a career,' and he adds : ' This surely indicates that hitherto he had dwelt mainly elsewhere.' [1]   Now this means that Holmes' coming to London and his settling down to a career were synchronous, and that therefore they took place in the *Gloria Scott* year, which Blakeney himself places ' not *less* than four years previous to *The Musgrave Ritual* and more probably five years earlier. His own date (p. 47) is 1874, and this agrees with H. W. Bell's calculation that *The Musgrave Ritual* is to be placed in

[1] T. S. Blakeney: *Sherlock Holmes,* loc. cit.

September, 1878.[1] We thus find that Holmes
(being at the same time *in statu pupillari*) ' waited '
in Montague Street for work to come his way,
and filled in his ' too abundant leisure time ' with
studies, for *four years*, during which time he
handled only two cases.[2] To this lengthy period
he afterwards refers as ' all those months of
inaction.' This is meiosis indeed ! Twelve
months, even eighteen months, might be so
referred to, but surely, if he had really waited
four solid years, he would have said so. No ; we
cannot possibly admit this hypothesis ; Holmes
cannot have come to London before 1876 at the
earliest, and thus the theory of an undergraduate
course in London falls to the ground, the phrase
' came up ' to London acquires only a metro-
politan, not an academic significance, and the
problem of the length of Holmes' university
career remains unsolved.

And the problem is a very real one. It is not
only that Holmes' own reported statements are
ambiguous. There is also an awkward chronological difficulty, which will be better appreciated
when we come to deal with a later part of the
problem.

[1] *Sherlock Holmes and Dr. Watson*, pp. 12–16.
[2] But see Note, p. 4. In any case, it is evident that the
cases were few and far between.

Setting, therefore, the question of Holmes' residence in London aside for the moment, we must consider the rival claims of Oxford and Cambridge. It is, I think, evident from the text that the friendship with Victor Trevor was made at one of the older universities, and not in London : the bull-dog, the attendance at chapel and the reference to athletics as a major interest of university life all point to this conclusion ; moreover, Mr. Trevor, now in late life ' a J.P. and a landed proprietor,' would doubtless wish to secure for his son just those social and educational advantages which he himself had missed and which, in those days, Oxford and Cambridge were alone considered to bestow.

It also appears likely that the friendship with Trevor preceded the acquaintance with Musgrave, since, in the one connection, Holmes is shown almost entirely friendless, whereas in the other he has so far imposed his personality on his surroundings as to occasion talk among the men about his methods.

The crucial point of the *Gloria Scott* paragraph is now clearly seen to be the bull-dog. Father Knox has pointed out, with the unanswerable cogency which belongs to inside knowledge, that the animal would not have been allowed inside the college gates. Blakeney replies that this objection is not insuperable, since Holmes was probably living ' out ' at the time, and may have been bitten in the town. Now, if the university had been Oxford, and if Holmes had resided there for two years only, or if in any case the acquaintance with Trevor is to be placed in the *first two years* of Holmes' residence there, then this situation would have been altogether impossible. At Oxford, freshmen are at once allotted rooms in college ; they reside there for two years, and only move out into lodgings in the town at the beginning of their third year of residence. At Oxford, therefore, the biting of Holmes while on his way to chapel through the streets of the town could not possibly have occurred before his third year—unless, indeed, we are to suppose that Holmes was so piously minded as to attend voluntary evening chapels, which, from his habits of mind and thought, appears unlikely.

At Cambridge, however, the system is different.[1] There, the freshman is usually accom-

[1] ' The Student's first business on arriving at Cambridge will be to procure himself rooms. The Tutor will inform him whether any sets of rooms within the College itself are vacant, and if not, which of the licensed houses in the town can admit him. . . . At some of the Colleges room is made within the walls for the freshmen, by expelling the questionists, i.e., undergraduates of the fourth year, into

modated with lodgings in the town during his first year and even (if the college lists are full) during his second year also. It is at once obvious that this system makes it very much more difficult for a man of solitary habits and reserved disposition to make friends among the men of his own year than the Oxford system. It would, therefore, be quite in accordance with probability that Holmes should have remained friendless during his first two years at Cambridge, and it seems possible that what he actually said to Watson was something like this : ' He was the only friend I made in my first two years at Cambridge, when I was living out of college.' Watson, either misunderstanding this at the time, or noting with hasty abbreviation : ' Only friend —2 yrs. out college,' and subsequently misreading ' out ' as ' at,' may have introduced here the complication which has proved so puzzling to commentators. The possibility that ' at ' is a mistake for ' in '—referring to a friendless two years spent in residence inside the college is

lodgings ; but in the majority the freshmen are served last as being the last arrived, and in many cases have to wait more than one term for admittance. . . . Nor . . . does the student in lodgings taste the genuine flavour of College-life ; besides, he will generally be at a greater distance from Chapel, Hall, and the Lecture-rooms.' (*Student's Guide to Cambridge*, 1874).

tempting, but must, I think, be discounted. It is the first two years that would be friendless, not the last two ; and a *first* two years within the college walls would imply residence at Oxford : a hypothesis which we have already been obliged to set aside on account of the bull-dog episode.

But even if we allow the expression to have been correctly reported, it is just within the bounds of possibility that the contradiction between Holmes' statement here and his further statement in *The Musgrave Ritual* is only apparent. We shall consider this point more carefully when we come to examine the question of Holmes' academic studies. The really important matter is that Holmes was more friendless during the period of his acquaintance with Trevor than during his ' last years,' and that this friendless period coincided with his residence outside the college ; this state of things necessarily indicates that he was at Cambridge and not at Oxford.

(B) We now come to the important question of the length of Holmes' residence at Cambridge. The theory that he was only there for two years, adopted by Blakeney on the strength of the *Gloria Scott* passage, seems to be contradicted by the expression ' my last years at the University ' in *The Musgrave Ritual*. We must now see how far these two statements can be reconciled.

Now, from various considerations,[1] it appears practically certain that the date 1878 for the adventure of *The Musgrave Ritual* is correct. At this period, Holmes had seen nothing of Reginald Musgrave for four years, i.e., since 1874. Since their acquaintance was but slight, it is improbable that they had met since leaving the University; therefore both Holmes and Musgrave were still at Cambridge in 1874. When, and at what age did Musgrave go down? Certainly not later than 1876, for he himself states that since his father's death in that year he had been managing his own estates, which he could scarcely have done had he still been an undergraduate. In addition to this, he is ' member for his district.' Bearing this in mind, we shall be inclined to assign the earliest possible date and the latest probable age for his leaving college. If he had gone up to Cambridge in the usual way at about eighteen, remained for the usual period of a little over three years,[2] and visited Holmes four years later, he would be at most twenty-five to twenty-six at the date of *The Musgrave Ritual*, and it seems unlikely that he would be a Member of Parliament at a much earlier age than that. We will there-

[1] Admirably set forth by H. W. Bell, loc. cit.
[2] See below, p. 18 ff, for the usual period of residence at this date.

fore suppose that he went down not later than 1874.

We must now consider to what extent his college career overlapped that of Sherlock Holmes. From the description given of him (his aristocratic appearance, dandified dress, grave, quiet manner and so forth) we shall not be disposed to conclude that he was the kind of person who would have 'drifted into talk' with a freshman of his own college, still less have 'sucked up' (as the expression goes) to senior men in his own first year. The same thing may be said of Holmes himself. 'Distrust the fresher who goes about with third-year men' is a commonplace of university philosophy. It appears highly probable that between these two students there was not more than a year or so either way : and in fact, Holmes' own remarks in the *Gloria Scott* story [1] rather imply that if he could not mix much with the men of his own year he would not and did not mix with any others. For these reasons I find it impossible to accept Bell's suggestion that Holmes went up in 1873, while Musgrave went down in 1874. It seems more likely that at this time both were senior men, Holmes in his third year and Musgrave in his third or fourth.

[1] I, 375.

Dorothy L. Sayers

It is implied that Musgrave visited Holmes in consequence of the ' talk ' at the University about his detective methods. This talk took place during Holmes' ' last years,' and, had he not gone up till 1873, would have to be dated forward to 1875 or 1876, that is, one or two years after Holmes' last meeting with Musgrave. Although it would be possible for Musgrave to have heard about them from men who left college later than himself, the text makes it clear that he had personally taken part in these discussions [1] ; this statement therefore affords additional proof that Musgrave and Holmes were contemporaries.

(C), (D) We thus find ourselves obliged to put back Holmes' matriculation to October, 1871,[2] in order to make him a third-year man in June, 1874. Since he cannot well have been less than eighteen at the former date, this gives us either 1853 or late 1852 as the year of his birth, at latest. That it cannot have been very much earlier is suggested by the fact that in August, 1914, he is described as being sixty years of age.[3] This calculation agrees sufficiently well with that

[1] 'I understand, Holmes, that you are turning to practical ends those powers with which you used to amaze us.' (*The Musgrave Ritual*, I, 400).

[2] See below, p. 24 ff.

[3] *His Last Bow*, I, 1076.

16

of Blakeney,[1] who offers 1852–1853, with a slight
preference for 1852 [2]; Bell's date of 1854 [3] is
probably a trifle too late. We may adopt 1853 as
a *via media*.

The extraordinary internal chronology of the
adventure of *The 'Gloria Scott'* prevents us from
placing any great reliance upon it for the actual
dating of Holmes' career. The dates given by
Holmes [4] are clearly impossible. We are, therefore, again thrown back upon the external
indications given in the introduction to that
story and to *The Musgrave Ritual*. If we are
correct in concluding that the 'two years'
mentioned in *The 'Gloria Scott'* refer to Holmes'
first two years at college, we must suppose that
his acquaintance with Victor Trevor was formed
between October, 1871, and June, 1873. The
visit to Trevor's home took place in the first
month of the long vacation, so that we have
the choice between July, 1872, and July, 1873.
There is but little to guide us, but Holmes
distinctly says that he and Trevor became 'close
friends' by the end of the term in which the bull-
dog attacked him, and rather seems to imply

[1] Op. cit., p. 3.
[2] But see below, pp. 24 ff.
[3] Op. cit., p. [xx].
[4] As contained in old Trevor's MS. and apparently
accepted by Holmes.

that the invitation to Donnithorpe matured in the long vacation immediately following. The fact that Holmes was still living out of college inclines us to assign the episode to the end of his first year; on the other hand, the fact that he was already engaged on chemical research in London, together with the reliance placed by Trevor on his advice and assistance, afford a slight presumption in favour of the later date. Everything depends, however, on the precise date of Holmes' Matriculation, which we shall deal with when we come to consider the question of his Tripos.

In any case, Bell's date of 1875 is clearly too late for The 'Gloria Scott,' based as it is on the assumption that Holmes did not matriculate till 1873; he thinks, however, that the long vacation at the end of Holmes' second year is the likeliest; this brings it to 1873, the date selected by Blakeney. My own preference, after the maturest consideration, is for 1872. The earlier date makes still more hopeless hash of the *Gloria Scott* chronology; but this, in any case, is so indefensible that a little more confusion can scarcely confound it further.

(E) Some further light on the subject may be gained by a consideration of Holmes' probable course of studies at the University.

We know little of Holmes' parentage and early history. That he was of gentle birth is known, and that his financial position was somewhat straitened is proved by the fact that at the time of his first meeting with Watson in 1881 he was unable to afford the full rent of the rooms in Baker Street. We may therefore conclude that his father was not a rich man, and it is quite possible that he came up to Cambridge with a Scholarship at one of the smaller and less expensive colleges. If he was a Scholar, he would naturally be expected to aim at an Honours Degree, and, indeed, it would be surprising if a man of his exceptional ability were to content himself with a Pass.

At that date, the principal Triposes open to him [1] were : Moral Sciences ; Natural Sciences ; Law and History ; Theology ; Mathematics ; and Classics. Classics and Theology we may eliminate at once ; nothing could be further from his line of thought. Nor can his occasional allusions to the ancient philosophers be taken to show that he had worked for his Tripos in the Moral Sciences. They suggest rather a desultory

[1] We need not consider the Oriental Languages Tripos. Music is also ruled out ; his interest in the music of the Middle Ages dates only from 1895 (I,968), and was, like his violin playing, only a hobby.

c 2

acquaintance than any profound study, while (as Father Knox has pointed out [1]) a certain looseness in his terminology suggests that, although he occasionally indulges in philosophical speculation, he was not altogether familiar with the methods of Academic philosophy. His logical terminology has also been subjected to criticism.[2]

Mathematics may be excluded with equal certainty—not so much on account of the bent of his mind, which seems admirably adapted to the study,[3] but because of his statement that his ' line of study was quite distinct from that of the other fellows.' At that period, as subsequently, the Mathematical Tripos at Cambridge was the largest and most famous of all. In 1874 the students taking Honours in Mathematics numbered 111 as against 71 in the next largest Tripos (Classics), and it would be absurd to suppose that

[1] *Essays in Satire*, p. 169.

[2] The Moral Sciences Tripos comprised three papers each in Moral and Political Philosophy, Mental Philosophy, Logic, and Political Economy.

[3] It is true that in The ' *Gloria Scott* ' he appears to be incapable of performing a simple subtraction; but this disability is not rare among advanced mathematicians. However, the Mathematical Tripos demanded a knowledge of Astronomy, which, as we know, he did not possess, at any rate in 1881. By 1890, he had advanced so far as to be able to discuss with Watson the causes of the change in the obliquity of the ecliptic (I,478).

Holmes would not have found mathematical fellow-students in any one of the seventeen Cambridge colleges.

We are thus restricted to a choice between (*a*) Law and History, (*b*) Natural Sciences.

Law would, no doubt, have had considerable attractions for him. The old Law and History Tripos, abolished after 1874, comprised one paper each on Roman Law, Criminal Law, International Law, Legal 'Problems,' Jurisprudence and Real Property, and one on set books. The Law side was thus much stronger than the History side, which consisted only of one paper on Political History of Europe, and two on English History. It might be natural to ask : Could a student of History have been so ignorant of the period succeeding the Crimean War as to accept the ludicrous errors of date incident to old Trevor's account of his mis-spent youth ?[1] The answer is, that it is perfectly possible. Owing to the singular academic theory that no historical event is of the slightest importance until it has well-nigh passed from living

[1] The dates of the Crimean War and the Gold-Rush are in themselves correct; but Holmes seems to think that the War took place thirty years before the date of the *Gloria Scott* episode and ten years or so before his own birth, whereas he was actually born in, or just before, the Crimean year.

Dorothy L. Sayers

memory, the periods covered by the 1874 Tripos syllabus were confined to the years 1814–1830 for Political History of Europe, and those between the Norman Conquest and the death of King John for English History, while the Special Period of English History was 1647–1688. There was no general paper on either English or European History ; so that it is more than likely that a man taking this Tripos would remain in abysmal ignorance of every historical event subsequent to 1830. He appears, on the other hand, to have had some acquaintance with the period of the Great Rebellion of 1647, which just comes into the Special Period [1] (see *The Musgrave Ritual*). The Law and History Tripos was not a very popular one, numbering thirty-four candidates in 1874, so that we cannot altogether exclude it from consideration.

But when we come to the Natural Sciences Tripos, the probability becomes so very much stronger that it almost amounts to a violent presumption of fact. This is, *a priori*, the Tripos which we should expect Holmes to take, having regard to his habit of mind and his known attainments. The scope of the Tripos was exceedingly wide, covering (1) Chemistry, (2) Mineralogy, including Crystallography, (3) Geology and

[1] *The Musgrave Ritual*, I, 415–16.

Palæontology, (4) Botany, including Vegetable Anatomy and Physiology, (5) Comparative Anatomy and Physiology. Students were not, of course, expected to familiarise themselves with the whole of this monstrous syllabus; it was sufficient to show intimate knowledge of two, or even one, of the subjects, in order to obtain Honours, while the scope of each subject was to some extent restricted by the syllabus. The twelve general papers set for the Tripos were framed to contain, each, one or more questions on each of the five subjects, so that on each and every day of the Examination a student seeking Honours might devote himself to those branches of study with which he was best acquainted. From what we know of Holmes' interests, we should consider it likely that he would select Subjects 1 and 5. These subjects, moreover, carried the highest number of marks, being rated at 2,000 marks apiece; whereas only 1,200 marks were allotted to Geology, Botany and Mineralogy respectively.[1]

[1] Geology and Palæontology may be definitely excluded from Holmes' studies. It would be difficult to take a Tripos in these subjects without being aware that the earth went round the sun (*A Study in Scarlet*, II, 16). Watson says that Holmes' Anatomy was 'unsystematic,' this probably only means that it did not follow the system to which Watson was accustomed.

When we come to look at the number of students taking the Natural Sciences Tripos, probability becomes almost certainty. In 1874, only seventeen students faced this Gargantuan set of examination papers (comprising in all 168 questions, exclusive of the Practical Papers in Anatomy and Physiology, and Physics, Chemistry and Mineralogy), and these students were divided among six colleges only, eight being from St. John's, four from Trinity, two from Caius and one each from Clare, Sidney Sussex and Pembroke. An undergraduate from any other college who took this Tripos might well observe that his ' line of study was distinct from that of the other fellows.'

The examination for the Natural Sciences Tripos [1] was at that time held in the Michaelmas Term and might be taken by any student who had already passed the Previous, not earlier than his eighth and not later than his tenth term after entering college, supposing that he had kept his statutory terms of residence. If, therefore, Holmes had matriculated [2] in the Lent or Easter

---

[1] As also for Law and History.

[2] It may be advisable to remind the reader that the term ' Matriculation ' had, at this date, nothing to do with qualifying examinations. An examination was, indeed, necessary as a rule in order to enter the *College*, and after passing this, the student ' came up ' to Cambridge and

Term of 1871, he would have become eligible to take his Tripos in the Michaelmas Term of 1873. Since, however, we know that Holmes and Musgrave were together in 1874, it seems more reasonable to suppose that Holmes came up in the usual course at Michaelmas, 1871, and proceeded to his Tripos in his tenth term, viz., Michaelmas, 1874. Alternatively, it is possible that he came up in Lent or Easter, 1872,[1] and took his Tripos at Michaelmas, 1874, in his eighth term. In the latter case, his acquaintance with Victor Trevor would still date from 1872 or 1873, the affair of the *Gloria Scott* (1872 or 1873) occurring when he had been one or two or alternatively four or five terms in residence. If we accept this hypothesis, we may at a pinch reconcile the conflicting statements of *The 'Gloria Scott'* and *The Musgrave Ritual*, by reckoning eight

---

was entered on the College books. ' Being thus made a member of the College . . . the freshman has to be formally enrolled as a member of the University. This enrolment, which is called Matriculation, does not, however, take place immediately on commencing residence, but on the day after the division, that is, the first day of the latter half of the term ' (*Student's Guide*, 1874). The ceremony took place in the Senate House.

[1] This practice of coming up in the middle of the Academic year, though unusual, and discouraged by the University authorities, was occasionally adopted from motives of economy.

terms (spread over the three calendar years April, 1872, to December, 1874) in the one case as 'roughly' two years, and in the other as 'roughly' three years. This would also enable us to accept Bell's birth-year of 1854. See, however, the conclusion reached in (*b*) below.

We are now in a position to attempt a more precise chronology of Holmes' academic career. Possible alternative dates are inserted within brackets.

1853 (late 1852 or early 1854).	Birth of Sherlock Holmes.
1871, October (1872, January or April).	Holmes goes up to Cambridge.
1872 (1873) . . .	Holmes, while still living 'out,' makes the acquaintance of Victor Trevor.
1872 (1873), early July .	Holmes visits the Trevors.
1872 (1873), late September or early October.	Death of Old Trevor; conclusion of the *Gloria Scott* adventure. Trevor goes down.
1872 (1873), October .	Holmes moves into rooms in College and becomes acquainted with Reginald Musgrave. (See below (*a*).)
1874, December (March) [1]	Musgrave takes his Tripos and goes down.
1874, November–December.	Holmes takes his Tripos, either going down immediately or remaining up to complete a second course of studies. (See below (*b*).)

[1] See below: Note on Reginald Musgrave.

1875–6 .	.	.	.	Holmes engages in other studies. (See below (G).)
1876 .	.	.	.	Holmes takes up residence in London in Montague Street
1878, September .		.	.	*The Musgrave Ritual.*

(*a*) It is not perfectly clear whether or not Victor Trevor belonged to the same college as Holmes.[1] It is probable that he was a man of Holmes' own year or of the year immediately above him. In the latter case, Trevor would, in the ordinary course of events, be going down in 1873, and, if they both belonged to the same college, Holmes may have succeeded to Trevor's rooms. If, on the other hand, Trevor still had another year at the University, we may ask ourselves whether it was his account of Holmes' 'methods' that started 'talk' among the undergraduates. Attractive as this theory is, it seems improbable that either Holmes or Trevor would have entered into public discussion of events so painful as those attending the decease of Trevor senior. It seems more likely that Trevor went down after his father's death, whether he had completed his studies or not, and that Holmes' 'methods' were demonstrated to Musgrave and

---

[1] If so, he must have been cutting Chapel on the morning of his fateful meeting with Holmes, since the bulldog could not have formed part of the congregation.

his friends in some other, and more trivial, connection.

(*b*) Having reached this point, our next step is obviously to examine the published lists of Cambridge Honours men for the period under review, to see how far they support our contentions. Unhappily, the name of Sherlock Holmes does not appear in the Cambridge History of Triposes for 1874, or for any other year; and we are forced to conclude, either that some accident prevented him from actually sitting for his Tripos, or that the lists were compiled with a lack of accuracy very far from consonant with the dignity of an Academic body.[1] When we turn, however, to the Book of Matriculations and Degrees, we find that a T. S. Holmes, who matriculated at Sidney Sussex in the Michaelmas Term of 1871, was admitted to the Degree of Bachelor of Arts in the Michaelmas Term of 1875 and to that of Master of Arts in 1878. It is true that the Christian names are given as 'Thomas Scott,' but the 'Scott' may be an error, due possibly to transcription from the Tripos Class list, where the habit of translating Christian

---

[1] It is not pleasant to suppose that the malignant influence of Professor Moriarty extended as far as Cambridge, or that he could have brought about an extensive and retrospective falsification of the published lists. It is better to presume carelessness than venality.

names, where possible, into Latin occasionally gives rise to confusion.[1] The date 1875 obviously refers to the actual date of taking the degree and not to the date of taking the Tripos, the thirteenth term after Matriculation being too late for the latter activity. If this entry refers to Sherlock Holmes, he must have allowed a year to elapse between taking the examination and presenting himself for the degree—a course which is not unusual. If this is so, we must abandon the attempt to reconcile the expressions ' two years ' and ' last years,' and suppose that Watson did misunderstand what Holmes said to him. This is the solution which I, personally, prefer.

(F) It is tempting to identify Holmes with the Sidney Sussex man who obtained a First Class in Natural Sciences in 1874. Unfortunately the name differs, so that we have here either another error of nomenclature or a regrettable omission.

In this connection, we may examine the claims of Sidney Sussex to be Holmes' college. It is one of the smaller colleges, having only fifty undergraduates on its books in 1874, the only colleges with a smaller membership at that date being Magdalene (49), St. Catherine's (46), St. Peter's (45), Downing (40) and Queen's (37). Its room-

[1] As when Mr. G. (Giles) Brown appears as Mr. E. (Egidius) Brown, and the like.

Dorothy L. Sayers

rents were moderate, ranging from £7 to £16 p.a., as compared, on the one hand, with Clare (£3 to £15), and on the other, with Caius (£12 10s. to £25). It possessed a Laboratory, and offered, in addition to its Foundation Scholarships, twelve Junior Scholarships, on the Taylor Foundation, of £40 p.a., several of which were given in Natural Sciences. It also offered a Special Course in Natural Sciences, and in connection with this, an Annual Examination was held in Chemistry, Electricity and General Physics, carrying with it a Prize to the value of £20, which was awarded each year, if any candidate attained a high enough standard to merit it. It thus appears that, of all the Cambridge colleges, Sidney Sussex perhaps offered the greatest number of advantages to a man in Holmes' position, and, in default of more exact information, we may tentatively place him there.[1] Even if Holmes is not actually to be identified with the Sidney Sussex man mentioned in the 1874 Tripos list, the fact that there was one other student in his year and college reading for the same Tripos does not necessarily conflict with his statement that his line of study was distinct from that of the other fellows; the ' other

[1] Reginald Musgrave would, in that case, also be a Sidney Sussex man. See below : Note on Reginald Musgrave.

fellow' may have specialised in Botany or Mineralogy, and may, in addition, have been a disagreeable or rumbustious person with whom Holmes would not care to associate. Apart from the special facilities in Nat. Sci., the chief interests of the college appear to have been mathematical, while a large number of its scholars and exhibitioners were drawn from the sons of the clergy and from certain specified schools. These men would undoubtedly have interests in common, from which Holmes might find himself excluded.[1]

(G) The last question that remains to be decided is : What did Holmes do between taking his Tripos in November–December, 1874, and coming up to London in 1876 ? It is barely possible [2] that he remained for another year at Cambridge to complete a second course of study —possibly in medicine.[3] The fact (if it is a fact)

---

[1] ' The smaller the College is, the more likely it is that all its members, or at least all who are of the same standing, will be acquainted with one another, *if there be no marked disparity of previous education to keep them apart.*' (*Student's Guide to the University of Cambridge*, 1874 ; my italics). In Holmes' case there was obviously marked disparity of tastes and probably of education also.

[2] If, that is, we reject the ' two years ' theory.

[3] I am informed that Students studying medicine at Cambridge usually took the Natural Science Tripos, and while reading for it, took the first and second M.B.

that he did not take his B.A. till 1875 rather suggests, however, that he was elsewhere, and it seems exceedingly probable that he spent some time abroad. We know that he was able to quote German,[1] and that at sundry periods in his career he undertook investigations in France (*The French Government Case*, etc.) and Italy (*The Vatican Cameos*, etc.) and conducted negotiations with various foreign agents; and it seems impossible that he should have transacted all this delicate and important business with the aid of interpreters. The suggestion that he learnt to speak modern languages with the requisite fluency either at his Public School or at the University will not hold water for a moment. In all probability he passed the year 1875 studying chemistry and languages at a German University, with vacation trips to France and Italy, returning to England in December to take his B.A. and then proceeding (perhaps after a short holiday at home) to London to wait for clients in Montague Street.

examinations, completing the medical side of their studies elsewhere after taking the B.A. degree. They rarely completed the medical course, and qualified for the M.B. and B.Ch. degrees, under five years from matriculation. It seems on the whole unlikely that if Holmes had possessed a medical degree of any sort, Dr. Watson would not have known, and mentioned the fact.

[1] *The Sign of Four*, II, 192, 271.

BIBLIOGRAPHY

Cambridge : *Historical Register to* 1910.
Cambridge : *Book of Matriculations and Degrees*, 1850–1900.
The Students' Guide to the University of Cambridge, 1866 and
    1874 editions.

NOTE ON REGINALD MUSGRAVE. To the observations already made about this young man we may add the following :—

Although he was of the highest social position, there is no mention of his ever having been at a public school, and he states that he learnt Trigonometry with his ' old tutor.' The Trigonometry would be required for his ' Little-Go ' if he aspired to Honours in any Tripos, and was no doubt studied for this purpose, so that he probably went straight to college from a course of private tuition at home. This exclusiveness would account sufficiently for his choice of a small college, where he could work hard and be free from the social pressure of public-school coteries. The choice of Oliver Cromwell's college is perhaps curious in a man of such Royalist tendencies, but this objection is of minor importance.

Since he was destined for a political career, he very possibly read the Law and History Tripos. In this case, he would go up in October, 1871, and take his Tripos at the same time as Holmes, viz., December, 1874. This fits the other data very well. In October, 1878, Holmes would not have seen him for three years and ten months—roughly ' four years.' The theory receives some support from Musgrave's acquaintance with seventeenth century spelling and his interest in the period of the Great Rebellion, which was, as we have seen, the Special Period for the Law and History Tripos, 1874.

On the other hand, these interests may be referred to his family traditions, and his Tripos may have been Classical or Mathematical. The examinations for these were held in the Lent Term and could be taken not earlier than the ninth term of residence. In that case, Musgrave probably matriculated some time between October, 1890, and April, 1891, and would thus be about one year senior to Holmes, going down in March, 1874, nine months before him.

Medical Career and Capacities of Dr. J. H. Watson

HELEN SIMPSON

It is not what we know, but what we can prove.

THE HOUND OF THE BASKERVILLES

MEDICAL CAREER AND CAPACITIES
OF DR. J. H. WATSON

'In the year 1878 I took my degree of Doctor
of Medicine of the University of London.'
These words are part of the first sentence of *A
Study in Scarlet*; their prim matter-of-factness
shows us Watson as no doubt he was, a student
who gave his pastors and masters no anxiety.
With characteristic modesty he is silent concerning his achievements during these five years of
preparation, but two facts of great significance
emerge as it were by chance; first, that he took
the degree of M.D. London, an extremely difficult
one to obtain; secondly, that he held, for an
unknown period, the post of house-physician or
surgeon at St. Bartholomew's Hospital,[1] before
going on to further training at Netley with a view
to becoming an officer in the Army Medical
Department.

At once a contradiction becomes apparent,

[1] 'I recognised young Stamford, who had been a
dresser under me at Bart's' (*A Study in Scarlet*, II, 6). This
phrase implies that Watson had held one or other of these
positions, which professional slang abbreviates to 'house-
man.'

when we consider that such achievements indicate a considerable degree of distinction in the
profession of medicine, and that the Army
Medical Department was at that time regarded
as a dead end.[1] The black silk gown, and hood
of scarlet cloth lined with violet silk, is only
conferred, after the M.B. has been taken, upon
the presenter of a thesis of outstanding merit.
The hospital posts were, and still are, sought only
by ambitious men, awarded only to men of
marked competence. Watson evidently had his
foot upon the first rung of the ladder. What
impelled him to descend, to abandon ambition
for obscurity ?

We have no factual evidence whatever, and
must examine the matter by such fitful light as
psychology affords. We know, and unscrupulous
commentators have made the most of it, that
Watson took an innocent pleasure in denigrating
his own past. He claimed to have had an
experience of women extending ' over many
nations and three continents,' and though this
boast was made in later life, there is an earlier, and

[1] The duties of regimental medical officer in peace were
chiefly concerned with the inspection of latrines and feet ;
in war, these were extended to include the administration
of field dressings, the organisation of evacuation transport,
and the selection of appropriate sites for camps. (Parkes,
Manual of Practical Hygiene, p. 669.)

even more unguarded phrase,[1] which shows that
the tendency was strong even in youth.

His friends, of course, knew that these hints
were to be regarded as wish-fulfilments rather
than as documents with chapter and verse, but it
is possible that such talk, overheard by irrespon-
sible or malicious persons, may have laid him
open to suspicion and reproof. The morals of
their juniors are no concern of the seniors in a
hospital ; but we may, by no great stretch of the
imagination, visualise some frailer member of the
other sex making charges against Watson, either
with a view to blackmail or revenge, to which
his indiscreet talk would lend some colour of
probability. It is impossible to be more definite ;
Watson himself is silent, merely giving the undeniable facts of his early success with an account
of subsequent deliberate steps taken to quit the
country. We respect his reticence, and probe no
further, reserving for him our pity, and our
condemnation for some not impossible she.

It is interesting to note that one of the more
important features of the 1878 Exhibition in
Paris was an international congress of army
doctors, whose report the curious will find
numbered 15 of the series issued by the French

[1] ' I have another set of vices when I'm well.' (*A Study
in Scarlet*, II, 13.)

Ministry of Agriculture and Commerce.[1] In this we find a very complete discussion of the methods of first aid, transport of wounded, and eventual surgical treatment which the European armies of the period found appropriate and practical. Surgeon-General Sir Thomas Longmore, representing Great Britain, showed himself very rightly jealous of the hierarchy which should compose the medical unit in the field, and emphasised the necessity of keeping this unit together so that members of it might become aware of each other's capacities and limitations. Watson, who as a keen student, and one contemplating an army career, must surely have been aware of this report, may later have wondered on what facts Sir Thomas Longmore's statements were based when he found himself transferred hither and thither,[2] from the Northumberland Fusiliers to the Berkshires, all in the course of a few short months.

By June, 1880, he was attached to General Burrow's brigade, which was defeated at what Watson so rightly calls the 'fatal battle' of Maiwand.[3] At this action Watson was present in

[1] *Congrès International sur le Service Medical des Armées en Campagne.* (Paris, Imprimerie Nationale, 1879.)
[2] *A Study in Scarlet*, II, 5.
[3] Ibid.

40

his capacity of Assistant Surgeon, but had small opportunity to put in practice all he had learned at Netley and London. A bullet shattered a bone —presumably the clavicle—and grazed the sub-clavian artery ; an attack of enteric fever retarded recovery. Major Leigh Hunt [1] attributes the onset of this disease to the eating of unripe or over-ripe fruit, impure water, or intemperate habits. We may dismiss from our minds the latter cause, and suppose only that Watson's natural good judgment was overpowered by the silent temptation of some unsuitable tropic fruit.

His return to England and first association with Mr. Sherlock Holmes are recounted in his own inimitable style. They met, as was appropriate, in a laboratory, and at the very instant when Holmes, forgetting his usual caution, was an-nouncing the discovery of a reagent ' precipitated by hæmoglobin, and by nothing else.' [2] Watson rightly showed considerable caution in accepting this extravagant statement—scientifically extrava-gant, that is ; for until Holmes had experimented with every other possible substance it was not permissible to make such a claim—and contented himself with remarking : ' It seems to be a very

[1] *On Duty Under a Tropical Sun*, 1882.
[2] *A Study in Scarlet*, II, 10.

delicate test.' This tact was the cement necessary to their subsequent friendship and fame. Commentators who deny that Dr. Watson was a person of critical intelligence may well consider whether such an endowment would have earned him his present niche in literature.

It may with more truth be said that occasionally he exercised forbearance when he should rather have exerted authority. Watson was aware [1] that his remarkable friend had, almost from the first, used drugs to stimulate his unusual powers, and by the time that the adventure of *The Sign of Four* began he had been for several months, three times daily, resorting to the syringe. [2] When the companionship started in 1881 this use of cocaine was only occasional; but seven years later [3] Holmes' mantelpiece was littered with 'tobacco, syringes . . . and other *débris,*' and one new and disturbing fact is to be noted. Holmes had become, as many addicts do, neglectful of elementary precautions; the scrupulous investigator who in 1881 stuck plaster over a finger puncture with the words, ' I have to be

[1] Ibid., 14.

[2] *The Sign of Four*, II, 143. We are given the strength of the solution of cocaine employed, but not the capacity of the syringe. It is therefore impossible to assess the amount of Holmes' daily doses.

[3] *The Dying Detective*, I, 1005.

careful,' by 1888 was content to use an un-
sterilised syringe without so much as a preliminary
rub of spirit on the skin. Even a ' neat morocco
case ' is no sure guard against the germs which
convey sepsis.

It has been conjectured that this condition of
dependence on the drug was the result of the
breakdown which followed Holmes' exertions
in the Netherland-Sumatra case, in 1887. Holmes
worked alone on this difficult business, and at
prolonged tension—fifteen hours a day for two
months—without Watson's imperturbability and
good temper at his elbow. It is not surprising
that Holmes, with no safety valve, and lacking
that best stimulus, an audience,[1] should have
attempted alternately to spur and to calm his
energies by an immoderate use of drugs. Indeed
he had apparently become so dependent on them [2]
that nothing but an entire and violent change of
surroundings could have effected a cure.

Happily this was forthcoming. Professor
Moriarty's attack, with its subsequent three years

---

[1] Holmes abhorred the notion of popular applause ; at
the same time he found Watson's honest admiration and
amazement stimulating. ' It had become in some way
helpful that I should register and interject.' (*The Creeping
Man*, I, 1244.)

[2] ' That drug mania which had threatened once to check
his remarkable career.' (*The Missing Three-Quarter*, I, 809.)

of wandering,[1] gave a new and reinvigorated Holmes to the world. By 1897, the time of *The Missing Three-Quarter* case, the 'indiscretions' were only occasional, though Watson was 'well aware that the fiend was not dead but sleeping.' Henceforth, however, references to the habit fail, and we may take Watson's word for it that his strategy of gradual weaning had been entirely successful.

It has been objected that Watson during their first association did nothing whatever to check a proclivity of whose symptoms and consequences he was perfectly well aware, and this has been adduced as showing a certain weakness of character. But Watson's explanation of his lack of remonstrance [2] rings true, that he did not wish to irritate a person of such great powers ; he was only too well aware that Holmes, adversely criticised, could be an unpleasant companion. His vanity, in those earlier days, was almost pathologically sensitive, and his need of Watson not so well understood as later it became. He would have been perfectly capable of breaking up

[1] 1891–4.
[2] There was one remonstrance, when Watson put the case for self-control forcibly and with a note of authority. Holmes was not offended, but exerted his considerable charm to turn the conversation, and Watson did not resume the subject. (*The Sign of Four*, II, 144.)

their association had Watson taken a strong line. Another consideration is not to be neglected. Watson was not in good health, and probably felt quite unequal to tackling so delicate a problem; his leg was giving considerable trouble.[1] The case of *The Sign of Four* came to deliver (temporarily) Holmes from indulgence and Watson from the consequences of candour; and the ending of the case, which spelled triumph for Holmes, brought to Watson the joys of matrimony, and, more important still from the point of view of this paper, a practice.

This practice was in Paddington, a district sufficiently near Baker Street to allow of occa-

---

[1] Watson alleges as the cause of this a bullet which has been identified with that which entered his shoulder at Maiwand. An explanation may be found, however, in some conjectural version of the incident related by him to Miss Morstan, of the musket which looked into his tent at dead of night, and at which he fired a double-barrelled tiger-cub. (*The Sign of Four*, II, 162.) No doubt there was some fine confused shooting on this occasion.

This wound, the result of accident, was evidently far more serious than the shoulder injury for which he drew his pension. We find that it 'ached wearily at every change of the weather,' (*The Sign of Four*, I, 146) and 'throbbed with dull persistence.' (*The Noble Bachelor*, I, 225.) If in the course of time the origins of both became transposed in his memory, who shall blame him? Enemy jezail or British musket, the leg-wound was gained on active service, and Watson is generally so free from vanity that he may surely be allowed this little touch of bravado.

sional visits to Holmes between professional
calls. It seems probable that it was bought [1]
with some of the money realised from the sale of
Mrs. Watson's pearls, sent her as conscience
money by Thaddeus Sholto. It was in a declining
condition, though it had been prosperous, but
Watson's energy and conscientiousness soon set
it on the up-grade once more. He had succeeded
in gaining the interest and confidence of certain
officials of the Great Western Railway,[2] which
brought him considerable work of a nature
familiar from his army experience; accidents
mostly, we may suppose, among the *personnel* of
the station.[3]

Watson's next-door neighbour was also a
doctor,[4] though the two were not in partnership.
Possibly this neighbour, somewhat alarmed at
Watson's increasing popularity, made Watson a
good offer to buy him out; possibly the neighbourhood was too close to Baker Street for Mrs.

[1] The usual price would have been three years' earnings;
about £900 in all.

[2] *The Engineer's Thumb*, I, 201–2.

[3] 'I knew from experience that railway cases were
seldom trivial.' (*The Engineer's Thumb*, I, 202.)

[4] *The Stockbroker's Clerk*, I, 356. This gentleman is
probably the Jackson referred to in *The Crooked Man* (I,
441). Anstruther was the Kensington neighbour who
occasionally gave him assistance. (*The Boscombe Valley
Mystery*, I, 75.)

Watson's liking. More probably a combination of the two causes induced Watson to move to Kensington,[1] where he acquired a small practice (paying for it with the money received from Dr. Jackson) and settled down to make a steady and comfortable living.

We may, therefore, imagine him going about the work of a good-class general practice in conscientious attendance upon the epidemics, maternity cases, and accidents of well-to-do households. His experience as an army surgeon, though hardly calculated to be of material use to him in this capacity, must have lent him a certain romantic quality in the eyes of those to whose bedsides he was called. And though his bronze had long since faded—indeed, Mrs. Watson, in June, 1889, comments on his pallor [2]—he retained his soldierly moustache,[3] the habit of tucking his handkerchief into his sleeve,[4] and, in changeable weather, his limp.[5]

[1] Probably the change-over occurred in November, 1888. During this month (*The Dying Detective*, I, 1001) he was in rooms, no doubt while the Kensington house was being made ready. By June of next year he was fully installed in Kensington. I accept Mr. H. W. Bell's dating throughout.

[2] *The Boscombe Valley Mystery*, I, 75.

[3] *The Naval Treaty*, I, 502.

[4] *The Crooked Man*, I, 439.

[5] *The Sign of Four*, II, 146.

We are now to consider, at such length as space allows, Watson's capabilities as a doctor.

It was said at one time, entirely without justification, that the Army Medical Department, and in particular the Indian branch of it, was staffed by 'failures who could count.' The reference is to those regulation pills which, being easily portable, were preferred to liquid medicament by successive Army Councils of the past. These were numbered from 1 to 12, according as the ailment to which each was appropriate might be listed, and the Army Surgeon's diagnosis thus had a tendency to limit itself to ills for which the treatment was officially procurable. Watson, however, was the exception. He was no failure, though he undoubtedly could count. His observation was as sure as that of Holmes, though his deductive powers were not so acute.[1] His professional eye was sharp; witness his immediate perception of Dr. Grimesby Roylott's bilious condition,[2] and of Isa Whitney's 'pasty face, drooping lids, and pin-point pupils'[3]—an admirable picture of the drug addict.

[1] Holmes admitted as much in the dialogue in *The Speckled Band* (I, 194). 'You have evidently seen more than is visible to me.' 'No, but I fancy I may have deduced a little more.'

[2] Ibid., I, 185.

[3] *The Man with the Twisted Lip*, I, 124.

48

His competence is shown in almost every case where we see him professionally at work. There are, however, one or two exceptions. Victor Hatherley, arriving shortly before seven in the morning at his consulting-room, before he quitted Paddington, found him alert, and equally ready to cope with hysteria or the dressing of a wound,[1] but it may be urged that the glass of water poured from the carafe might have calmed Hatherley more successfully had it been thrown in his face as soon as he began his ominous laughter; and in the patient's already excitable condition a hot drink rather than alcoholic stimulant might seem more appropriate. It must be remembered, however, that at such an hour of the morning—a little before seven o'clock—a hot drink would not have been readily available. The actual bandaging was competently done.

Objection has been made to his description of Jefferson Hope's aortic aneurism[2] as being somewhat too sensational. 'An extraordinary throbbing and commotion'; 'a dull humming and buzzing noise'; these seem in fact exag-

---

[1] *The Engineer's Thumb*, I, 203–4.
[2] His discretion veils the fact that this kind of aneurism is generally a consequence of syphilis. Jefferson Hope himself attributed it to exposure. (*A Study in Scarlet*, II, 122.)

gerated expressions. But it must be remembered that Watson was speaking as a doctor, to whom the implications of any considerable variation from the normal heart-beat were at once apparent; these phrases therefore must not be taken as his impression of actual sounds, but of sounds whose significance as danger signals he could only convey by some exaggeration in speech.

It might be expected that Watson should have detected the deception by which Neville St. Clair simulated a twisted lip. He and Holmes saw the man for the first time together, when Watson, with his customary quickness (military experience aiding) diagnosed the deformity as a weal from some old scar.[1] It was no fair test, however; his observation was made through the grating of a cell, and at a distance certainly of seven or eight feet.[2]

Another instance of spot diagnosis, where the data are insufficient to allow us to judge whether or no he was right, is that of a boy of fifteen, who as the result of 'a fall in childhood' had acquired a twisted spine, but could run, and was evidently

---

[1] *The Man with the Twisted Lip*, I, 145.
[2] 'The prisoner lay with his face towards us.' (Ibid., I, 145.) This implies that his feet were nearest the door at which the watchers stood; the head would therefore be at least the length of the bed away.

active. Watson's words are, ' a curious shambling gait which told my surgical eyes that he was suffering from a weak spine.'[1]   Watson is always careful not to use expressions which may puzzle the layman, but these simplifications make interpretation difficult for the commentator. Had he used the words ' ataxic gait,' we might have known that the boy suffered from some congenital syphilitic affection ; had he spoken of a ' spastic gait,' we should have pictured some such trouble as that which afflicted Byron.   A gait showing signs of paralysis of one or more groups of muscles is probably what he meant, but he is evidently mistaken in suggesting spinal injury as the cause.   Any injury sufficient to affect the walk would certainly not permit the boy to ' rush,' and would be far more likely to involve complete paralysis below the waist.

However, Watson undoubtedly did keep up with medical research as well as his health and the calls of a practice would permit ; we hear of him reading the *British Medical Journal*,[2] plunging furiously into the latest treatise upon pathology,[3] and find him deep in a recent treatise on surgery.[4]

---

[1] *The Sussex Vampire*, I, 1191.
[2] *The Stockbroker's Clerk*, I, 354.
[3] *The Sign of Four*, II, 158.
[4] *The Golden Pince-Nez*, I, 783.

He was also aware of Dr. Percy Trevelyan's work on obscure nervous lesions; a work which, though unpopular in its published form,[1] was sufficiently well considered by his professional seniors to gain him the award of the Bruce Pinkerton prize and medal. Watson, of whom Holmes remarked in connection with his diagnosis of lumbago in the matter of *The Creeping Man*,[2] 'You always keep us flat-footed on the ground'— what was Watson doing with a work on obscure nervous lesions?

He was, moreover, familiar with the work of the French psychologists of the period, a fact which comes out, appropriately enough, in the *Adventure of the Six Napoleons*. This, too, at first sight, appears an odd study for a man in general practice, until we come to consider his close association with Holmes. He could not hope to rival the energy of that mind, almost encyclopædic in the extent of its interests; but he might humbly aspire to supplement Holmes' knowledge or memory should occasion arise. And in fact these difficult and abstruse studies, this secret labour, did justify itself. To Lestrade's request for an opinion Watson was able to respond with

[1] 'My publishers give me a most discouraging account of its sale.' (*The Resident Patient*, I, 460.)
[2] *The Creeping Man*, I, 1250.

a brief lecture on monomania, the *idée fixe* ; and
we may imagine something of a triumphant eye
cocked at the listening Holmes, who, by no means
well-pleased at the display, snubbed it down in an
instant. ' That won't do . . .' ' Well, how do
you explain it ? ' ' I don't attempt to do so.' [1]
We know Holmes' vanity, we know how he
would resent even so slight a turning aside of the
limelight ; and we may respect Watson's endea-
vour, though it met with no very generous tribute
from his friend.

It is less unexpected that he should have been
aware of the presence in London of ' Dr. Ainstree,
the greatest living authority upon tropical
disease,' at the time (November, 1888) of Holmes'
presumed illness.[2] Watson cannot have spent
quite twelve months in India, but the lure of the
East had evidently been strongly felt by him.
He was still upon half-pay, and may have
cherished the not too fantastic hope of one day
being allowed to return there, not as a regimental
medical officer, a post from which his limp would
debar him, but in some more sedentary capacity.
He therefore kept up his knowledge of tropical
medicine, possibly attended post-graduate lec-
tures, and even though his acquisition of **a**

[1] *The Six Napoleons*, I, 742.
[2] *The Dying Detective*, I, 1004.

practice put an end for the time to any prospect of further army service, the interest persisted as a habit.

It is sad, when Watson at this period showed such immediate and sure knowledge of the greatest resources of contemporary medicine,[1] to find him, less than ten years later (February, 1897) confessing he had so lost touch with his profession that the name of Dr. Leslie Armstrong was unknown to him.[2] Dr. Armstrong was, it appears, a Cambridge professor with a European reputation in more than one branch of science. The confession is not so humiliating as might at first appear. Professors, unlike prophets, are honoured chiefly in their immediate neighbourhood, and a European reputation may very well be attained without the fact impinging on the consciousness of a general practitioner whose tastes do not happen to lie in the direction of those branches of science in which it has been gained.

Watson's capabilities in the matter of first-aid are next to be discussed. Here there is a great quantity of material, all of it showing him at his best. His dressing of Victor Hatherley's thumb has been dealt with; there follow in chrono-

[1] 'Let me bring Sir Jasper Meek or Penrose Fisher, or any of the best men in London.' (Ibid.)
[2] *The Missing Three-Quarter*, I, 82

logical succession the cutting down of Beddington,[1] with its subsequent artificial respiration;
the reviving of Mr. Melas[2] with the aid of
ammonia and brandy; of Miss Barnet,[3] roused
from opium poisoning by strong coffee; of Lady
Frances Carfax,[4] whose recovery from chloro-
form poisoning was effected by means of artificial
respiration and ' every device that science could
suggest,' including the injection of ether; of
Dr. Huxtable,[5] on whose lips brandy was
rubbed; and lastly, the attempt to ameliorate the
sufferings of Baron Gruner[6] by bathing his face
in oil, covering the raw surfaces with cotton
wadding, and injecting morphia. These examples
show that Watson was more than adequate as a
general practitioner, prompt in emergency—' in
an instant ' he had caught up Beddington to take
the pressure from his neck—tactful, and with the
gift of holding his tongue. It is difficult to
conceive of an individuality more likely to
succeed in general practice.[7]

---

[1] *The Stockbroker's Clerk*, I, 369.
[2] *The Greek Interpreter*, I, 496.
[3] *Wisteria Lodge*, I, 916.
[4] *Lady Frances Carfax*, I, 1039.
[5] *The Priory School*, I, 662.
[6] *The Illustrious Client*, I, 1115.
[7] Blessington's question, ' Have you the tact ? ' (necessary for a successful doctor) could certainly have been

Helen Simpson

I come now to the much-discussed incident[1] of the deception practised by Holmes upon Watson in the matter which involved the arrest of Culverton Smith. It is not for me to pronounce upon the right or wrongs of this deception; those casuists who insist that the end may justify the means will certainly approve the device employed by Holmes. Fortunately, it is my business to confine myself to that aspect of the matter which shows Watson as a doctor; and here, once more, he is displayed as an ornament to the profession.

It has been said that he should at once have perceived the truth. Holmes' appearance and character had been intimately known to him for years; Watson was aware that his friend could simulate illness,[2] and was not above playing a practical joke. But when the circumstances are fully considered this objection cannot hold. Watson saw his friend in a dark room, made still more obscure by fog. He was never allowed to

answered by Watson in the affirmative. (*The Resident Patient*, I, 462.)

[1] *The Dying Detective*, I, 1000 *et supra*.

[2] 'It is a very easy complaint to imitate. I have done it myself.' (*The Resident Patient*, I, 470.) This remark was made just over a year previous to the incident under discussion. Also see *The Reigate Squires*, I, 437, for Holmes' sham fit, which occurred in April, 1887.

turn the gas up past a half-light, nor to approach the bed for examination. Holmes was an artist in make up, and the lips crusted with beeswax, eyes dilated with belladonna, and cheeks lent a fever by rouge must have been very convincing at a distance. Also, the psychological point should be stressed that Watson came prepared, from Mrs. Hudson's recital, to find a genuinely sick man.

It has been urged that Holmes' questions intended to demonstrate Watson's ignorance—' What do you know, pray, of Tapanuli fever? What do you know of the black Formosan corruption?'—did in fact serve their purpose. Not so; Watson's answer, the answer of an honest man, was the correct one. ' I have never heard of either.' Of course he had not; they had no existence. Holmes probably knew of the studies in tropical medicine and was playing upon his friend's vanity, which happily was not so great as his integrity. A doctor less professionally honest might have pretended to having heard of this pair of imaginary diseases; it never occurred to Watson then, or at any other time, to pose.[1]

Apart from doing the impossible, that is, seeing

[1] We must except his harmless vanity in the matter of the leg-wound.

through a deception carried out with all the power of Holmes' intelligence, and backed by the actual fact of three days' starvation, Watson's behaviour in this instance was perfectly justifiable. He could not insist that a doctor should attend upon Holmes; it is the inalienable right of the Englishman to die without medical attention if he so desires. He had seen how any kind of opposition infuriated the patient, and was wise to agree to a request that seemed comparatively rational, that he should send for a man familiar with the disease which his friend supposed had struck him down. True, not even in the course of his tropical studies had he heard the name of Culverton Smith quoted as that of an authority;[1] but since, on Holmes' own showing, Smith was not a qualified medical man, this silence on the part of the orthodox of the profession is fully accounted for. No doubt he felt, setting out on his errand, that it would be better if Holmes were to die according to the rules of medicine; on the other hand, he was aware that miracles are more often to be hoped for from quacks. It says much for his feeling for Holmes that it was allowed to transcend, in this matter, loyalty to his order; and it should be remembered that by associating

[1] *The Dying Detective*, I, 1007.

himself with an unqualified person, by meeting such a person in consultation, he ran the considerable risk of having his conduct called in question by the General Medical Council, with possible disciplinary measures to follow.

This incident shows Watson in a most favourable light. His behaviour throughout is typical of his sterling honesty as a doctor, and his devotion as a friend. It is not the final incident of his professional life, but it is an important one, and as such it has been reserved for the end of this paper, so that elbow-room might be allowed to it after other matters had been cleared.

One or two points concerning the Kensington practice may be given in conclusion. It was bought late in 1888,[1] and seems at first to have repaid his diligence. But from one reason and another it appeared thenceforth to decline, so that we find such statements as : ' I have nothing to do to-day. My practice is never very absorbing,' [2] and ' The practice is quiet,' [3] succeeding each other as the years go on. We may suppose that the strain of Mrs. Watson's long illness, which seems to have begun soon after their marriage, and which ended with her death, had

---

[1] See p. 8.
[2] *The Red-Headed League*, I, 43.
[3] *The Final Problem*, I, 545.

something to do with the half-hearted manner in which, after his first enthusiasm and busy years, he allowed the practice to go to pieces. Eventually, when loneliness and his own shattered health obliged him to abandon it, it was bought by a distant relative of Holmes, Dr. Verner,[1] for an amount which is not stated, though it was the highest price that Watson ' ventured to ask.' Since the money for the purchase was provided by Holmes [2] who, unworldly as he was in the matter of payment for his services, could certainly at this period (August, 1895) command high fees when he chose, we may assume that it was not less than Watson had given in the first instance, i.e., about £1,000.[3]

This about exhausts the information concerning his work as a general practitioner in London. Its value in his life was, as he would be the first to admit, by no means equal to that of his association with Holmes. Watson the medical

---

[1] *The Norwood Builder*, I, 584.

[2] Ibid.

[3] The Paddington practice was bought for £900, and presumably sold for a little more ; Watson had improved its value during his short tenure. For his ' small practice in Kensington ' he probably paid the amount he had received from Jackson ; and the highest price he would venture to ask seven years later would certainly not be more.

man could, despite his brilliant beginnings, never have aspired to any position of world-wide consequence ; Watson the biographer is second only to the greatest names. We cannot regret the turn of fate which left him solitary in London, to exist as he could upon eleven and sixpence a day, since it resulted in so rich an experience as this friendship, an experience in which his powers of narrative have made us sharers. We recognise, and are beginning to pay, our debt.

The Limitations of Sherlock Holmes

VERNON RENDALL

His ignorance was as remarkable as his knowledge.

A STUDY IN SCARLET

THE LIMITATIONS OF SHERLOCK HOLMES

A *Life of the Apostles* by Judas Iscariot might be a favourite model for the fashionable biographer of to-day. I have no desire to be up-to-date in denigration; but it is as well to see a great man as he was, making some allowance for the rose-tinted spectacles of the patient Watson. A god and a worshipper make a complete religion, and this is the position of Watson the humble follower with regard to his idol. He describes Holmes as ' the best and the wisest man whom I have ever known.' [1] ' Best ' perhaps, as having done so much good work, though Holmes would not touch humdrum cases. But ' wisest '? In this description, doubtless unconsciously, Watson is echoing the last words of the *Phaedo* of Plato concerning Socrates. Holmes could never claim to be a philosopher. I do not see him, like Socrates, standing in the street lost in meditation, or talking freely to everybody. Socrates could go into battle as a common soldier and deserve the

---

[1] *The Final Problem*, I, 556.

award for valour, and he could take an intrepid part in the politics of his troubled democracy. The maxim which Holmes quotes, ' *Vox populi, vox Dei,* '[1] would not have satisfied him. News of a revolution, a possible war, or an impending change of government did not interest Holmes,[2] though he explains that at times his own brother *is* the government.[3] Mrs. Hudson was a great improvement on Xanthippe, and Socrates had, so far as one can judge, some of Holmes's indifference to women. They are, on the whole, keener observers than men, and they might have taught him something, as Irene Adler did. He kept her photograph, but made no effort to get into touch with other women equally gifted. Even Socrates had his Diotima and consulted her on love, which Holmes treated with a gibe and a sneer.[4] His utter lack of appreciation, when feminine beauty and charm were presented to him, is a grave defect. Lacking this source of distraction, he became so bored with life, when not engaged on a case, that he took violently to drugs, and had to be weaned away from them by Watson. Cocaine three times a day for many

[1] *The Abbey Grange*, I, 858.
[2] *The Bruce-Partington Plans*, I, 968.
[3] Ibid., I, 970.
[4] Plato, *Symposium*, 201D ; *A Scandal in Bohemia*, I, 3.

months[1] might easily have led to hallucinations. In *The Illustrious Client*, a story of events in the year 1902, Holmes says of the beastly Baron Gruner: ' A complex mind. All great criminals have that. My old friend Charlie Peace was a violin virtuoso.' [2]

This reference is rather disconcerting. For Holmes, one thinks, if he had any lengthy acquaintance with Peace, must have noticed his abnormal and degenerate face, his absences at night, owing to his perpetual burglaries, and his possession of fine things beyond his apparent means. Even if his false arm with a hook remained hidden, his way of life would suggest suspicion. The solution of these difficulties is that, unless Holmes was in the North of England in his 'teens,[3] he would not have come across Peace. It was only after the Bannercross murder that Peace came to London and evaded capture as Mr. Thompson, of Peckham. He shaved off his white beard, dyed his hair, stained his face with walnut juice, and wore spectacles. His left hand, however, had one or more amputated fingers. Hands, according to him, the police did not

---

[1] *The Sign of Four*, II, 143.
[2] *The Illustrious Client*, I, 1094.
[3] I rely on a colleague more learned in the Holmes-chronology than I am. See Miss Sayers' article (above, p. 26).

F 2

notice, though they looked at the face he was able
to distort. Holmes did notice hands,[1] and if he
had indeed recognised the skulking murderer,
would surely have delivered him up to justice.
Holmes was never on the wrong side.[2]

Peace's active career, not always under his own
name, was before Holmes began his professional
practice as a detective, and I take it that he
referred to Peace as an ' old friend ' because he
was familiar with all the famous trials of the
century. He remembered well a case of 1875.[3]
Peace began his large experience of prison in 1859,
and in 1876 actually attended the trial in which
another man was convicted of a murder to which
Peace himself subsequently confessed. It should
be added that in general he was too plausible a
rogue to speak the truth when it did not pay him
to do so. Therefore, many details of his life
are uncertain. We do not know definitely how
long he continued his musical performances in
public, though they seem to have ceased in his
boyhood.

Quoting, like Watson, the *Satires* of Horace,[4]

---

[1] See *The Red-Headed League, A Case of Identity, The
' Gloria Scott,' The Solitary Cyclist*, etc.

[2] *The Final Problem*, I, 543.

[3] *The Resident Patient*, I, 476.

[4] *A Study in Scarlet*, II, 139.

one might say to Holmes : ' You can't be an hour
by yourself or make a proper use of your leisure.'
This leisure cannot, really, have been very
extended, unless, as I suspect, Holmes had a habit
of sitting up late at night and doing then what
he might have done during the daytime. For
consider the labour and time involved in keeping
up to date the records of his cases in the large
Year-Books, and that ' great index,' or common-
place-book, which included notes on Vipers, a
circus dancer, and foreign Vampires, in the ' V '
volume.[1] This ' encyclopædia of reference ' contained biographies of peers and of criminals, and
to keep their stories accurately, with changes of
residence, additions, and losses, must have
required perpetual writing. Holmes read several
newspapers ; he was well acquainted with the
social and official scandals of the late Victorian
era ; he kept an eye on Continental crime [2] ; and
he missed nothing in the Agony Column, or
Columns.[3] What about the arrangement of
items from these various sources ? He put them
in order ' only once in every year or two ' ; but
he did spend an autumn day in making cross-

[1] *The Sussex Vampire*, I, 1178–9.
[2] *The Illustrious Client*, I, 1091.
[3] *The Three Garridebs*, I, 1201–2. But apparently he
skipped the sports columns (see *The Missing Three-Quarter*).

references.[1] Only those who have kept common-place-books for years can realise the labour of cutting out, pasting in, and indexing from day to day or from month to month.

All this gathering of data is a lengthy business, and might have occupied much of the day that Holmes found tediously empty. To scrutinise *The Times* alone carefully takes an hour. The collection of oddities would be extensive. Thus the double question whether men with wooden legs could be physically capable of violent crime [2] and were inclined to it would lead to the preservation of such cases as I have noted in the London area within a brief period at Woolwich, Hackney, Dulwich, and the Docks. Besides this work, Holmes was a composer [3] and critic [4] of music, as well as a performer on the violin, an attendant at operas,[5] concerts,[6] and art galleries,[7] and a writer of monographs which must have taken considerable time to put together.[8] Why, if he

[1] *The Musgrave Ritual*, I, 397.
[2] *The Sign of Four*, II, 168, 183, 235.
[3] *The Red-Headed League*, I, 45.
[4] *The Bruce-Partington Plans*, I, 968.
[5] *The Hound of the Baskervilles*, II, 454; *The Red Circle*, I, 968.
[6] *A Study in Scarlet*, II, 44, 45; *The Red-Headed League*, I, 45.
[7] *The Hound of the Baskervilles*, II, 315.
[8] *A Study in Scarlet*, II, 19–21, 38 (see also *The Sign of*

was bored, could he not have added another, say, on *Disappearances in London*? His range of reading outside business is obscure, and may have been freakish. It included three modern languages.[1] Certainly he had little time for such reading, as he was often busy with chemical experiments.[2] His delving in old English charters [3] might have been endless, and he might have been expected to specialise in English genealogy, in which he shows a marked interest.

And why, one asks, did he not lighten his gloom by playing some game? Chess with Watson, a patient loser, would have occupied many hours. Dr. Johnson commended cards,[4]

Four, II, 147, and *The Boscombe Valley Mystery*, I, 97); *The Hound of the Baskervilles*, II, 282; *The Bruce-Partington Plans*, I, 996, 1000; *The Cardboard Box*, I, 937; *The Dancing Men*, I, 630.

[1] He quotes French (*The Sign of Four*, II, 190; *The Red-Headed League*, I, 55), German (*The Sign of Four*, II, 192, 271), and refers to his 'pocket Petrarch' (*The Boscombe Valley Mystery*, I, 84). His work for the French Government (*The Final Problem*, I, 357) and for the Pope (*The Hound of the Baskervilles*, II, 289; *Black Peter*, I, 697) presupposes a good practical knowledge of French and Italian.

[2] *A Study in Scarlet*, II, 7–11, 14; *The 'Gloria Scott,'* I, 380; *The Naval Treaty*, I, 500; *A Case of Identity*, I, 69.

[3] *The Three Students*, I, 763.

[4] Holmes did, indeed, on one occasion, give proof that he could play whist (*The Red-Headed League*, I, 50).

Vernon Rendall

which occupied the leisure of Gibbon ; Napoleon
played chess ; and I have seen a learned Professor
absorbed in tiddlywinks. There is billiards, too,
which most men, including Watson, have some
idea of,[1] though golf had hardly arrived in
England at the end of the nineteenth century.
Holmes could fence and box,[2] but he looked
upon ' aimless bodily exertion as a waste of
energy.' [3] This neglect of healthy pastimes is a
singular limitation both in Holmes and in Watson.
He who cannot play at something with somebody
is not fitted for life. Watson, I suspect, was
intimidated out of his natural turn for games by his
dominating friend, who preferred inconvenient
and solitary revolver-practice within doors.[4] The
great man was an epicure ; he rated his own
society above that of other people. ' You have
never yet recognised my merits as a housekeeper,' [5] Holmes remarks to Watson. So he
took a part in the buying of the household,

[1] Watson, of course, played (*The Dancing Men*, I, 611).
Holmes seems to have smoked a cigar in the billiard-room
at Donnithorpe (*The ' Gloria Scott,'* I, 378), but that he
played may be doubted.
[2] *The ' Gloria Scott,'* I, 375 ; *The Yellow Face*, I, 334 ;
The Sign of Four, II, 175–6.
[3] *The Yellow Face*, I, 334.
[4] *The Musgrave Ritual*, I, 396.
[5] *The Sign of Four*, II, 226.

though not necessarily the whole of the ordering. The friends may have done it by turns. Holmes' alternation of ascetic eating and good food seems eminently sensible. Johnson wrote that 'very few men know how to take a walk.' Holmes could walk with Watson—once, indeed, for two hours.[1] Watson had brilliant periods of silence, and unlike Holmes he could find things in houses that were worth looking at. Holmes had no appreciation of Nature, and only in his later years acquired some regard for the country scene,[2] taught doubtless by Watson, who never failed to notice the glory of gorse and the colours of autumn. To the same influence we may attribute the reading of J. G. Wood's *Out of Doors*, which solved one of Holmes' latest cases.[3] He would have done well to leave flowers alone till he could talk sense about them. Bursting into a lecture on a rose, he ignores the elementary fact, for students of natural history, that colour and scent are not 'extras' in blossoms.[4] They are designed to attract the insects which fertilise them and so help to produce the seed. Alone among great men, Ruskin adopted a similar

---

[1] *The Yellow Face*, I, 334.
[2] *The Final Problem*, I, 551.
[3] *The Lion's Mane*, I, 1285.
[4] *The Naval Treaty*, I, 513.

standpoint when he noticed flowers—he was too pure to think of seed.

Holmes shows some acquaintance with the Latin,[1] French [2] and German [3] classics, but knows nothing of Greek and Greek texts. The story of *The Three Students* contains deductions founded on supposed facts which to a classical scholar are ridiculous. I have suggested elsewhere that this case is really Watson's masterpiece, got up to

[1] He refers to Horace (*A Case of Identity*, I, 75), and quotes him (*A Study in Scarlet*, II, 139). He quotes Tacitus (*The Red-Headed League*, I, 32). In the guise of an old bookseller he offers Watson a Catullus (*The Empty House*, I, 564).

[2] He quotes Boileau (*A Study in Scarlet*, II, 54); La Rochefoucauld (*The Sign of Four*, II, 190); and Flaubert (*The Red-Headed League*, I, 55).

[3] He twice quotes Goethe in the original (*The Sign of Four*, II, 192, 271), and refers to Jean Paul Richter (ibid., 203). In this connection, it is strange that Mr. T. S. Blakeney (*Sherlock Holmes : Fact or Fiction?* p. 14) should regard ' Jean Paul ' and ' Richter,' mentioned on the same page, as different persons. Watson got at Jean Paul through Carlyle, and Mr. Blakeney might, with a minimum of trouble, have perceived that both references are to the same person. Richter explains in his unfinished *Autobiography*, which is available in English, the origin of his two names, John Paul, and promises to tell his readers why he adopted ' Jean Paul ' as a pen-name, first used in his *Unsichtbare Loge*. He did not give the promised explanation ; but, as Ernst Förster suggests in the biography attached to Vol. XVI of the *Collected Works* in German, the pen-name was doubtless intended as a tribute to the French culture from which he had learnt so much.

keep Holmes amused when he was feeling the lack of his home and his usual occupations.[1]

Other detectives are always monotonously the same and are never out of sorts. Holmes is much more human. He can be depressed, he can get ill, and he can get angry. Watson, the worshipper, observes after the Return that he has not lost his asperity of temper.[2] His vanity, which is described as 'small,'[3] is huge, and he himself confesses to 'an impish habit of practical joking,'[4] and a desire to create a dramatic surprise. He insists on startling a man who is out of health.[5]

He likes to keep his discoveries to himself until the last moment, a reticence which, in the case of the phantom Hound, caused the death of an escaped convict and very nearly that of Sir Henry Baskerville as well. Like a god he plays special Providence, and lets off criminals who would get a very different reception from the English law.[6] He recognises that revenge is a kind of wild justice.[7] He does not, however,

[1] *The London Nights of Belsize*, 1917, pp. 147–57.
[2] *The Empty House*, I, 573.
[3] *The Sign of Four*, II, 146.
[4] *The Mazarin Stone*, I, 1158.
[5] *The Naval Treaty*, I, 531.
[6] *The Abbey Grange*, I, 858.
[7] *Charles Augustus Milverton*, I, 738.

indulge in the moral remarks of which coroners are fond. His name, ' Sherlock ' belongs to several divines of note, two of whom were well known as controversialists. A trace of this influence may be seen in his remark that religion ' can be built up as an exact science by the reasoner.' [1] It is likely that one of his parents was excessively interested in religious questions, if indeed a Sherlock was not an admired ancestor in the family. He reacted against this early dose of religion and seldom, as the saying is,' improved the occasion.' For the ordinary reader this is a blessing, though others may regard it as a fault.

His stoic suppression of emotion is very plain, and, as Watson says, he was ' undoubtedly callous from long over-stimulation.' [2] His letter, when at death grips with Moriarty, was written, we may conclude, in one of his rare moments of perturbation, though his hand was firm and clear. It includes the detail, ' I made every disposition of my property before leaving England, and handed it to my brother Mycroft.' [3] This is somewhat obscure. Does he mean, ' I have made a will and handed it to Mycroft,' or, since ' property ' is the last noun mentioned, ' I have

[1] *The Naval Treaty*, I, 513.
[2] *The Valley of Fear*, II, 469.
[3] *The Final Problem*, I, 556.

conveyed my property to my brother'? Considering what Watson had done for him, his omission from a will would be rather surprising; but it would be in accordance with the practice of solid English people, who have a way of leaving their money in the family and forgetting the friends who have made their lives possible and agreeable. But in any case, Holmes, though wishing Watson for a while, at least, to suppose him dead, might later have sent him privately news of his survival. He has the grace to apologise to Watson for this mistrust. The will, if made, was presumably proved. But when Holmes reappears Watson says nothing about having received a legacy, which he would surely have done, with the remark that his friend had not forgotten him. When Watson was wanted, his doctoring had to give way. In condonation of such insistent claims, however, it must be observed that Holmes had probably taken the chief part in financing the joint establishment in the days before Watson's marriage. His payments to Mrs. Hudson were 'princely,' [1] and he gave secretly the first price which Watson asked for his Kensington practice. [2] Though his charge for

---

[1] *The Dying Detective*, I, 1001.
[2] *The Norwood Builder*, I, 584.

cases was fixed,[1] he certainly made a lot of money[2] ; but he also worked gratis or took only his expenses.

Vanity prevents him from acknowledgements which would have been gracious—to Poe's *Gold Bug,* for instance, in *The Musgrave Ritual.* Vanity, too, makes him so egocentric that he deplores any word in Watson's narratives not devoted to his deductions.[3] Contemporary comment on the immortal pair shows that Watson was right in his methods. The details which Holmes regarded as superfluous are now eagerly scrutinised, and a bare, unadorned statement of deductions, such as Holmes preferred, a story with no attention to character or to the detail which makes a scene convincing is found to be tedious. Is it not so with some later chroniclers of detection? The public will weary of clues long drawn out and a superfluity of red herrings, and will demand some real people for a change, people who have passions, feelings, and bad habits.

Admirable as are Watson's powers of narrative, he was somewhat blind as a worshipper, and he

---

[1] *Thor Bridge,* I, 1221; but this was perhaps said in order to put off a client whose manners he disliked.

[2] *The Final Problem,* I, 539.

[3] *The Sign of Four,* II, 145 ; *The Copper Beeches,* I, 275–6 ; *The Blanched Soldier,* I, 1117–18.

was bluffed more than once by conclusions which will not stand close examination. 'The Science of Deduction,' at the opening of *The Sign of Four*, contains a faulty example. Watson has gone out to a post office and must, Holmes argues, have sent a telegram, because he has not written a letter and has postcards and a sheet of stamps in his desk.[1] Watson agrees to this as evident and undeniable ; but equally well he might have gone for a money order or a postal order, to inquire the cost of sending a parcel to India or Australia, or to buy stamps of a different value to those contained in his sheet.

The deduction of a man's age from his handwriting is certainly a very doubtful matter. I do not believe that ' in normal cases one can place a man in his true decade with tolerable confidence.'[2] This statement is not confirmed by my experience with a host of contributors writing for two papers for many years. Watson is asked to delight in the traces of heredity shown by the p's in a document made by a father and a son writing alternate words.[3] There are only two of them, and to me they seem tolerably different. The period at which a hand becomes fixed varies

[1] II, 148.
[2] *The Reigate Squires*, I, 434-5.
[3] Ibid., I, 438.

widely, but, once settled, it remains unchanged
for many years, though ill-health or excitement
may introduce marked changes.[1]

Experts do not believe that a large head
necessarily indicates unusual brain-power. I
remember an old friend who had an abnormally
big hat, and a big brain underneath it, saying that
the biggest head he knew belonged to a singularly
stupid man. Yet from a large hat Holmes makes
the inference, ' of course obvious upon the face
of it,' that its owner is ' highly intellectual.' [2]
The conclusion that a woman who wears gold
pince-nez must be well dressed is unconvincing.[3]
People, when they first buy glasses, know
nothing of their price, and the vendor naturally
provides them with the most expensive form of
eye-wear. Vanity also induces them to have gold
fittings, and they may insist on a detail which
concerns their face, even if they cannot run to
good clothes. Forty years ago, it must be
remembered, horn spectacles had not come into
fashion, and glasses, being regarded as a dis-
figurement, were not so often worn as they are
to-day. Gold-rimmed glasses may have been
bought during a period of prosperity which in

[1] See R. L. Stevenson : *The Wrong Box*, ch. VI.
[2] *The Blue Carbuncle*, I, 153.
[3] *The Golden Pince-Nez*, I, 791-2.

later life their owner no longer enjoys. Was not this the case of the Russian woman who came over to seek her husband ? It seems doubtful if she had sufficient resources to dress well. Others besides Lord Robert St. Simon [1] wear golden eye-glasses. As I write, a notice appears in the papers of a woman with gold-rimmed glasses whose dull, if not slatternly clothing, as described, resembles that of a charwoman rather than what is prescribed by the ' dictates of fashion.' This last specimen of commercial English expresses the feminine horror of being out of date in clothes. Doubtless every woman dresses as well as she can afford, or even better.

One curious limitation in Holmes' methods has always surprised me. At the British Museum in his early days he acquired useful knowledge,[2] but not, apparently, later. It is odd, since he admired the work of Bertillon,[3] that he did not discover the important paper which Galton gave to the British Association in 1899 on *Finger-prints and the Detection of Crime in India*. Galton's method was examined by a committee appointed by Asquith, in 1894. Holmes is tepid in his reply to Lestrade's

[1] *The Noble Bachelor*, I, 231 (also John Openshaw : see *The Five Orange Pips*, I, 105).
[2] *The Musgrave Ritual*, I, 399.
[3] *The Naval Treaty*, I, 522.

question on the subject. He has ' heard something of the kind.' [1] That is all. Finger-prints as a means for detecting criminals were first used by Sir William Herschel of the I.C.S. in the district of Hooghli, in Bengal. They were recognised as superior to Bertillon's anthropometry, and were recommended for all India in a report of 1897. All one can suggest is that Holmes was not eager to take up other people's methods. With his vanity, he found it difficult to use another expert to help him.

It is plain that the resources of the ideal detective should be equal to every contingency.[2] Billy the page says : ' Mr. Holmes always knows whatever there is to know.' [3] But Holmes did not reach omniscience ; no more does anybody else. With a vast memory, he had acquired the art, which many people lack, of using it effectively at the right moment ; and, after all, his knowledge was immense, particularly in odd directions where the ordinary man and the policeman are at a loss. He would have been among the first to recognise that use of hyoscine which made Crippen so popular a character with the public.

The details which I have noted are no dis-

[1] *The Norwood Builder*, I, 601.
[2] *The Five Orange Pips*, I, 115–16.
[3] *The Mazarin Stone*, I, 1141.

paragement of his remarkable powers. If he sacrificed everything, Watson included, to his work, he may have been justified by the results he obtained.[1] He should be compared not with Socrates, but with a masterly egotist like Gibbon the historian, who concentrated his life and energy on work he could do better than anyone else. Cæsar and Napoleon had each to tackle an impossible state of affairs. The answer to those who object that their ideas of reconstruction were faulty is that no one else could have done the job at all, and that therefore their methods had to be accepted. So with Holmes. His foibles had to be tolerated or ignored, because no one else could produce his results. His personality and his gift for drama remain unequalled. Thirty years since, the references to his name in the Press exceeded those due to any author. He was above Shakespeare, even above Dickens, who was always popular with journalists for being able to supply a little humour at a pinch. That pre-eminence, like frock coats, hansoms, cheap tobacco, drinks for the three-mile traveller, and the De Reszkes, is gone. The art of quotation and reference to the classics has decayed in the twentieth century.

---

[1] ' " *L'homme c'est rien—l'œuvre c'est tout,*" as Gustave Flaubert wrote to George Sand,' is Holmes' own remark at the end of *The Red-Headed League.*

G 2

Vernon Rendall

But Holmes and his Boswell remain objects of
intense interest, and none of the crowd of
imitators who have been created by their success
has made anything like a similar impression on
the world.

The Singular Adventures of Martha Hudson

VINCENT STARRETT

Mrs. Hudson, the landlady of Sherlock Holmes, was a long-suffering woman.

THE DYING DETECTIVE

THE SINGULAR ADVENTURES OF
MARTHA HUDSON

It rained in London through the night of
March 3rd, 1881 ; by the morning of the 4th
the streets were sloppy and depressing. Some
fog was abroad, and ' a dun-coloured veil hung
over the house-tops, looking like the reflection
of the mud-coloured streets beneath.' [1]   An
Acherontic sort of morning, all in all ; and to
Mrs. Hudson, standing at her window, at No.
221B Baker Street, it may well have seemed that
something harrowing and revelatory was about
to happen—or indeed was in the act of happening
all round her. That disturbing consciousness of
singular events in prospect and proximity ! For
some weeks now she had been mildly wondering
about her curious lodgers ; in particular the tall
one, with the thin hawksbill of a nose and eyes
set close together in a high-domed head.

Conceivably, she only shrugged—observing
that the day was cloudy—and turned her attention
to something in the oven. But if the mood of

[1] *A Study in Scarlet*, II, 27.

doubt existed it must have deepened by the
morning of the 5th. By that time the impending
drama had begun to run its course. Used as
she was becoming to the nondescript individuals
who visited Mr. Sherlock Holmes, she had not
until that morning set eyes upon the Baker Street
division of the detective police force; and the
sudden intrusion of half a dozen disreputable
street Arabs must have given the good woman
pause. Their pattering footsteps on the stairs
were accompanied by audible expression of
her disgust.¹ What thoughts, one wonders,
did she at that moment think about her principal
lodger?

Thereafter came Gregson, of the Yard, taking
the long flight three steps at a time, after almost
pulling out the doorbell; and on his heels the
sallow, rat-faced Lestrade, his garments untidy
and disarranged. And then, immediately, the
significant request of Dr. Watson for the sick
terrier. To Martha Hudson, below stairs, it must
have seemed that odd events were transpiring
in the chamber overhead. One fancies her, at that
moment, plump and puzzled, standing beside the
stair-foot. Her dark brows are met in a frown
as she cocks her best ear upward. She is bending
forward, her hands upon her hips. Does she

¹ Ibid., 54.

catch a fragment of the conversation? Perhaps the strident voice of Sherlock Holmes, pausing in his eternal tramping up and down the room?

'*There will be no more murders!*'[1]

Then, as she waits and listens, again the door-bell rings. It is young Wiggins, the leader of the ragged urchins, come with the missing cabman. Each in his turn mounts upward, and the door of destiny closes behind them. At the stair-foot Martha Hudson sniffs and turns away; then stops, appalled.

A crash has sounded from the room above that seems to shake the building. Feet pound upon the floor and cries of fury filter through the ceiling. A desperate struggle is in progress, marked by every evidence of violence. And Martha Hudson, cowering against her door-frame, listens to the deadly scuffle with consternation and dismay. Her blood has turned to water and she is weak with terror; yet in her bewildered mind she checks the values of furnishings now crashing to the floor against the possibilities of their replacement by the villains responsible.

Ought she to send for the police? Yet Gregson and Lestrade were of the police, as possibly she may have known. One views her there, upon that morning—frightened, indignant,

[1] *A Study in Scarlet*, II, 70.

Vincent Starrett

with heaving bosom and disordered mind, waiting the final, unpredictable catastrophe. An obscure, heroic figure on the outer rim of terrifying drama. Good soul, her direst secret fears at length have been realised. She had always known, one thinks, that something terrible would happen with that man in the house. And mingled perhaps with her alarm there is a little sense of satisfaction—of fearful triumph—that her predictions have been fulfilled.

In some such fashion, at any rate, must Mrs. Hudson, housekeeper to Sherlock Holmes and Dr. Watson, have come to a clear knowledge of her principal lodger's profession. There is no record that she was ever told ; and if she was, she can have had—until that terrific episode—no notion of what the simple words portended. Watson himself had been told only the day before. One hopes that Holmes, on his way downstairs with the prisoner, a little later, stopped long enough to allay her natural fears ; and it is likely that he did, since he and Watson were permitted to remain upon the premises. There can be little doubt that Holmes made good the damage wrought by Jefferson Hope.

In this first instance of the dangerous nature of the detective's employment, as it touched her own existence, Mrs. Hudson may well have sensed a chapter of adventures that would have frightened an ordinary woman into another line of business. It is perhaps a permissible deduction that already for some years she had been letting out her rooms to curious customers, and was not unacquainted with the difficulties of the London landlady. However that may be, it has long been certain that she was not an ordinary woman. A young widow, one imagines her to have been, who took up commercial housekeeping when the experiment of marriage was in some way tragically ended. But no whisper of her life before that day in 1881, when Holmes first called upon her, has ever been revealed. The notion persists that she had been unhappy; she kept so very still about it all.

That first occasion taught her, we may suppose, what she might expect of Sherlock Holmes. Yet some time was to elapse, one thinks, before he actually ventured upon revolver practice in his living-room—decorating the wall with ' a patriotic V.R. done in bullet-pocks '[1]—and it is probable that this diversion was not too frequent. A certain *rapport* would seem to be indicated, as between the two, before such queerish pastimes could be tolerated—an understanding based on faith and works ; at least, a feeling of certainty

[1] *The Musgrave Ritual*, I, 396.

on the part of Martha Hudson that her curious lodger was able and willing to pay for a new wall, if necessary. Other and various scenes of violence and disorder must have occurred to prepare her for that first patriotic fusillade ; yet even so it must have come upon her with a sense of shock. Loud voices, heavy falls, the crash of glass and table furnishings, even the noisome odours of experiments usually conducted in a laboratory— such matters may become in time part of the casual daily routine of existence ; but shooting is always a little dangerous and startling.

One faintly wonders about the living-room wall. That it was a substantial piece of building is rather certain : solid beams of oak, perhaps, under a paper about whose pattern, save for Holmes' shooting, Watson has chosen to be reticent. It seems unlikely, however, that Holmes—a man of an original turn of mind— confined himself to a single set of initials, however appropriate. There were other monograms, no doubt, which Watson simply failed to mention. Mrs. Hudson, we may be sure, mentioned them on numerous occasions before the rattle of her lodger's patriotic gunfire became familiar.

But in time she probably told herself—and others—that nothing now that Mr. Holmes could do would ever surprise her. After the first episode of the Boxer cartridges there can be little doubt that she was prepared for anything. And one fancies that she came in time to like the perilous uncertainty of her position. There are persons who live with equanimity upon the slopes of a volcano, enjoying the threat of danger that hangs over them. After an eruption they return and build their homes anew, upon the very spot from which they were dislodged. So, possibly, it was with Mrs. Hudson. And, too, she was a part of that never-ending operation against the forces of evil—a reflection in which, as an honest woman, she must have found some satisfaction. Even some pride.

One does not minimise the genuine affection she came in time to have for Holmes and Watson ; an affection shared, as she may have suspected, by some millions of the doctor's readers, any one of whom would have been happy to change places with her. And if her orderly soul was dismayed by cigars in the coal-scuttle and tobacco in the toe-end of a Persian slipper,[1] her protests in time, we may be certain, became mere humorous sallies which were responded to in kind. The sight of the detective's unanswered correspondence, transfixed by a jack-knife in the centre of his

[1] *The Musgrave Ritual*, I, 396.

wooden mantelpiece,[1] may have distressed her
in the early days of his probation; but such
vagaries—after a year or two—probably troubled
her less than they troubled Watson, who had to
live with them.

Her habits, at the beginning of the relationship,
were probably more or less fixed. They changed,
perhaps, or were adapted to her lodgers', as the
years wore on. Apparently she went to bed
about eleven, an hour after the maid. Waiting
for Holmes to return from his pursuit of the
mysterious old crone, in the course of the
Lauriston Gardens investigation, Watson heard
her ' stately tread '[2] as it passed the living-room
door. And presumably she rose early enough to
satisfy Holmes and the doctor, who were not
notoriously early risers. For all of them, it is
clear, 7.15 was a bit unearthly, on a cold spring
morning. It was at that hour, early in April,
1883, that Watson blinked up at Holmes from his
warm island of bed-clothing and learned that Miss
Helen Stoner had arrived from Stoke Moran, on
the western border of Surrey.

Holmes obviously felt that an apology was in
order: ' Very sorry to knock you up, Watson,'
he said, ' but it's the common lot this morning.

[1] Ibid.
[2] *A Study in Scarlet*, II, 50.

Mrs. Hudson has been knocked up, she retorted upon me, and I on you.' [1]

But Mrs. Hudson had been affable enough; she had hurried down to light the fire and boil a pot of coffee. Watson, good fellow, was inclined to be a trifle curt until he had his coffee, a circumstance that possibly she remembered.[2]

During the evenings she was visited by her cronies. How numerous these were we cannot be certain ; but they were numerous enough for a ring at the doorbell, on a stormy night, to suggest one such—rather than a client—to Sherlock Holmes. His conjecture that John Openshaw, whose ring had interrupted an evening of cross-indexing, was ' likely to be some crony of the landlady's,' [3] was not, of course, borne out by fact ; but it was a significant remark. No landlady is without her cronies, and we may be certain that the landlady of Sherlock Holmes had cronies by the score. Her tales of her astonishing lodger, and his companion, must have made good telling for the shivering, envious women who sipped at tea or coffee with Mrs. Hudson—did they call her 'Udson ?—of No. 221B Baker Street. Watson

[1] *The Speckled Band,* I, 173.
[2] *A Study in Scarlet,* II, 19.
[3] *The Five Orange Pips,* I, 104.

himself, one ventures, told no more harrowing stories of prowess and of peril than Martha Hudson to her satellites.

Her staff, during the early days, was not a large one. There was a servant—alternatively called 'the maid'[1]—and just possibly a page in buttons ; or it may be that the page was taken on a little later. His first recorded appearance, viewing the narratives in their chronological order, is in Watson's account of *The Yellow Face*,[2] an episode dated in the month of April, 1882. It is possible that he was employed some months after the advent of the detective and the doctor, at a time when the increasing number of visitors, calling upon Mr. Sherlock Holmes, too frequently snatched the maid and Mrs. Hudson from their necessary household duties. Just conceivably he was a bit of swank on the part of Mrs. Hudson, who may well have looked forward to a time when she could afford a page, like other and more prosperous landladies. However that may be, he is not to be confused with a later page, called Billy, for whom Holmes entertained a considerable affection.

The establishment, then, was relatively small,

[1] *A Study in Scarlet*, II, 50 ; *The Five Orange Pips*, I, 120 ; *The Bruce-Partington Plans*, I, 969.
[2] I, 334.

and in all charity one cannot imagine Mrs. Hudson or her maid to have been overworked. There were no other lodgers, we may be sure, at any time. Had there been others, Holmes would surely have complained of them (or they of him), and we should have some record of them in Watson's pages. Holmes and Watson themselves, of course, made work enough, but Mrs. Hudson's labours cannot at any time have been excessive. The famous living-room, after all, was somewhat sacrosanct. From time to time, no doubt, the maid was allowed to enter—possibly under the watchful eye of Mrs. Hudson—for an imperative cleansing; but this would be only when the sternest necessity demanded it. Watson, in all likelihood, was agreeable enough to intrusion; but Holmes would not have cared to have domestics messing up his household gods. That the chamber was perennially untidy is one of the soundest of our certainties.[1] One fancies Watson as making shift to keep the place in order, but there is a clear record of his despair. The principal duties of the maid then, upstairs, it may be ventured, was making up the beds.

Throughout all of the Watsonian text there is the distinct suggestion that Mrs. Hudson did the

[1] *The Musgrave Ritual*, I, 396–397; *The Dying Detective*, I, 1000.

cooking. Holmes bragged a little, in *The Sign
of Four*, about his ' merits as a housekeeper,' [1]
but it was Mrs Hudson, one feels certain, who
prepared the oysters and the grouse. They were
to be ' ready in half an hour.' [2] Holmes merely
ordered them from the shop—presumably while
wearing a disguise described by Watson as
suggesting ' a respectable master mariner who
had fallen into years and poverty.' [3] And it was
quite certainly Mrs. Hudson who prepared the
woodcock, during the excitements of the detective's search for the Blue Carbuncle. In view of
the circumstances of that curious adventure, it
will be remembered, Holmes thought of asking
her to examine the bird's crop. [4] This, to be sure,
was after Watson had left his companion for a
wife ; but there is small reason to suppose that
Mrs. Hudson gave over the task of cooking after
the doctor's departure. Holmes dined at seven,
in those days, he told his friend, when inviting
him to return, [5] although in point of fact it was
considerably later before they actually got around
to woodcock.

This admirable bird, incidentally, would appear

[1] *The Sign of Four*, II, 226.
[2] Ibid.
[3] Ibid., 223.
[4] *The Blue Carbuncle*, I, 160.
[5] Ibid.

to have been a favourite with Holmes. Among
the ingredients of the 'epicurean little cold
supper' arranged by him for Lord Robert St.
Simon and the Moultons, some years earlier,
were a 'couple of brace of cold woodcock, a
pheasant, a *pâté-de-foie-gras* pie, with a group of
ancient and cobwebby bottles.'[1] Mrs. Hudson
had no hand in that proceeding, however; the
dishes were from a confectioner's. They arrived
during the detective's absence, greatly to the
surprise of Watson. It is, of course, conceivable
that Mrs. Hudson was away during the afternoon
and evening of this event; but a more likely
explanation is that Holmes—often a singularly
thoughtful man—did not care to burden her with
such an extensive and luxurious repast. It is also
conceivable that he did not believe her quite up
to such a spread: a supper for a noble bachelor
is, after all, a supper for a noble bachelor.
Sherlock Holmes had his own idea of Mrs.
Hudson's abilities in a culinary way. In the final
episode of *The Naval Treaty* she rose to an
occasion and produced, in addition to ham and
eggs, a dish of curried chicken for Percy Phelps'
breakfast. 'Her cuisine is a little limited,' the
detective testified on that occasion; 'but she

[1] *The Noble Bachelor*, I, 240.

has as good an idea of breakfast as a Scotch-
woman.' [1]

On the whole, it would appear that Mrs.
Hudson was at her best where a breakfast was
concerned ; her staples were ham and eggs, with
toast and coffee.[2] These she prepared entirely to
the liking of her lodgers ; and, as we have seen,
she was capable of rising to an occasion. When
something more elaborate than curried chicken
seemed to be in order, Holmes took the matter
into his own hands and some confectioner was
benefited. Nevertheless, she could prepare the
traditional roast of beef,[3] and did occasionally
prepare it ; it stood, when cold, upon the
collaborators' sideboard until, presumably, they
indicated that they were through with it. Fortunately for Holmes there was a cold joint on hand
during his investigation of the disappearance of
the Beryl Coronet.[4] It saved him from going
hungry throughout an arduous afternoon and
evening.

But it is to be remembered that Holmes and
Watson frequently dined out. In particular was

[1] *The Naval Treaty*, I, 530.
[2] *A Scandal in Bohemia*, I, 25 ; *The Engineer's Thumb*, I,
205 ; *The Naval Treaty*, I, 530 ; *A Study in Scarlet*, II, 19 ;
The Sign of Four, II, 211.
[3] *A Scandal in Bohemia*, I, 18.
[4] *The Beryl Coronet*, I, 266.

this likely to be the case after some rather special triumph; and the strong probability is that Mrs. Hudson prepared no dinners without previous orders. If Holmes planned to dine at home one evening, no doubt when possible he told her of his intention. When he failed to leave instructions, he took pot luck from the sideboard or hunted up a restaurant. 'Dinner for two as soon as possible,' was his order at the conclusion of the adventure of *The Mazarin Stone*,[1] but it was probably something from the sideboard.

Tea was, from time to time, a pleasant possibility in the day's events, but for the most part the two men were well occupied from breakfast through to dinner, and even later. From the point of view of Mrs. Hudson the arrangement, all in all, may not have been the best imaginable; but in the circumstances it was the only arrangement possible.

Complicating even the simple routine of breakfast was the fact that Holmes rose fairly late, save when he was roused untimely, while Watson rose conspicuously later. Frequently as we see the friends together at the breakfast table—a pleasant tryst, and a favourite scene with most of the doctor's readers—it was actually not often that they entirely synchronised. Often Watson

[1] I, 1158.

came down to find Holmes gone about his business; and at best it was his habit to enter the scene to the last rattle of his companion's coffee-cup. Triumphant indeed must have been an occasion when Watson finished before Holmes; one such is recorded in the opening lines of *The Hound of the Baskervilles*.[1] Sherlock Holmes, as we behold him, is still seated at the breakfast table, while Watson stands upon the hearth-rug, examining the handsome stick left by Dr. James Mortimer the night before. Obviously he has already finished, and in the warm glow of comfortable satiety he dares to venture some pregnant observations of his own.

But the whole business of breakfast must often have been a little trying for Mrs. Hudson.

Years later, the faintest possible clue emerges from Watson's text to indicate a change in the Baker Street domestic staff. In the opening scene of *Thor Bridge*, dated by inference in the early days of October, 1900, two hard-boiled eggs suggest to Sherlock Holmes a certain division of interest on the part of a new cook.[2] A *new cook*—the words are clearly printed in the record. But a new cook suggests an old cook, now vanished from the scene. And the original cook was

[1] II, 275.
[2] I, 1216.

certainly Mrs. Hudson. It is a disturbing hint ; and it is obvious only that somewhere along the years a cook was taken into the household, who was in turn supplanted by another. The probability is that the first one appeared at a time when Mrs. Hudson believed herself to be becoming prosperous. Somewhere along in 1888, perhaps ? By that time—we have Watson's word for it— Holmes' payments to his landlady had become quite ' princely.' [1]

There is much for which we must always be grateful to Watson. He told what seemed to him important. But it never crossed his mind that we should ever care to know the exits and entrances of Baker Street domestics. Yet as more and more the interest of the world centres upon the life of Mr. Sherlock Holmes, every item of his association becomes enchanting. It is possible to regret the doctor's reticence about the humbler lives that toiled obscurely in the echo of that sonorous reputation.

About the page, for instance. He had his uses. He held the door for those who had business with Mr. Sherlock Holmes, and for those with whom Holmes had business. He held the door for clients entering and prisoners departing. It was an exciting enough existence for a lad. Two

[1] *The Dying Detective*, I, 1001.

pages, at least, are indicated during the public career of the detective, and the last and best of them was Billy. His first appearance, unless Watson is confused, was some time prior to the adventure called *The Valley of Fear*, in which episode, as recorded, he is already on the job. It was Billy, we are told, who showed Inspector MacDonald into the collaborators' living-room.[1] That was in January, 1887; and as late as the summer of 1903—a long stretch—he was still apparently upon the premises. In that year and season he greeted Watson, in the opening scenes of *The Mazarin Stone*, and made a significant remark. Watson, noting the dummy of the detective in the window, observed, according to the record : ' We used something of the sort once before'[2]—an obvious reference to the adventure of *The Empty House*,[3] which occurred in April, 1894. And Billy replied that *that* had been before his time.

It is immediately evident that Watson *was* confused when he recorded the circumstances of MacDonald's arrival in 1887. In this matter we may safely trust to Billy, who would have a clearer memory of his employment than would the doctor. Unless, indeed, the earlier page was

---

[1] II, 467.
[2] I, 1142.
[3] I, 571-582.

also called Billy; in which case it is difficult to
see how the problem can be settled without
greater confusion than already exists. In *The
Noble Bachelor*, however, one of Holmes' cases
that followed *The Valley of Fear* by only a few
months, it was 'our page-boy,'[1] in Watson's
words, who threw open the door to announce
Lord Robert St. Simon; there was no mention
of any Billy. Nor was there in the earlier record
of *The Yellow Face*,[2] an odd mystery that came to
Holmes in the spring of 1882. But it was clearly
Billy who, on October 4th, 1900, ushered Mr.
Marlow Bates into the presence.[3]

The actual change of pages took place, one
fancies, some time after the adventure of *Shoscombe Old Place*, which occurred in the early
summer of 1897; in Watson's account of that
curious episode the page-boy is still nameless.[4]
The final proof would seem to lie in the doctor's
record of 1903, at which time Billy was still 'the
young but very wise and tactful page, who had
helped a little to fill up the gap of loneliness and
isolation which surrounded the saturnine figure
of the great detective.'[5] In spite of the 'third

[1] I, 230.
[2] I, 334.
[3] I, 1220.
[4] I, 1302.
[5] *The Mazarin Stone*, I, 1140.

person ' form of narrative, the quoted words are
too clearly Watson's own for any doubt to exist
about their authorship. It is notorious that by
January, 1903, he had remarried, and the com-
placent utterance is precisely what he would have
thought about the predicament of Holmes, after
a few months of separation.

But in spite of the presence of a page upon the
premises, it was Mrs. Hudson herself who
frequently announced the detective's visitors.
There must have been some system about the
matter, a private one that functioned consistently
but without conscious thought, perhaps, in her
interesting mind. Class consciousness, one thinks,
had some bearing on the matter. Martha Hudson,
a loyal and devoted servant of an indubitably
higher type, was unquestionably a bit of a snob.
Her exclamations of disgust, twice recorded,[1] at
the boisterous entrance of the ragged urchins led
by Wiggins, are sufficient in themselves to urge
the point ; but it is her conduct in the instances
of distinguished visitors that betrays her. These
she ushered up the stairs herself, and bowed them
through the door. The case of Lady Hilda
Trelawney Hope is typical [2] ; her card preceded
her, majestically, upon the brass salver. And

[1] *A Study in Scarlet*, II, 54 ; *The Sign of Four*, II, 212.
[2] *The Second Stain*, I, 869.

immediately before the Lady Hilda there had
been the illustrious Lord Bellinger himself—
' twice Premier of Britain.' [1] Such things were
always happening. Watson would have been
' guilty of an indiscretion '[2] if he had even hinted
at the identity of some of the illustrious clients
who crossed the humble threshold in Baker
Street, during the one year 1895. There is small
question that Mrs. Hudson handled all such in
person.

If the King of Bohemia appears to be an
instance to the contrary—he climbed the steps
in solitary splendour and rapped authoritatively
on the door—it is to be remembered that, for all
the richness of his attire, he was a rather terrifying
figure, even for *fin-de-siècle* London ; and it is
probable that he snapped on his black vizard
mask a little earlier than Watson thought. The
doctor's deduction that he had adjusted it outside
the living-room door, because ' his hand was still
raised to it as he entered,' [3] is plausible and
ingenious, but not necessarily the fact. He may
simply have been testing it for security at that
highly secret moment. To Mrs. Hudson he may
well have seemed some wild bandit from the
Balkans.

[1] Ibid., 860.
[2] *Black Peter*, I, 696.
[3] *A Scandal in Bohemia*, I, 9.

As summing up this amusing situation in the household, it may be suggested that where visitors or clients were of sufficient importance to warrant her personal attendance, Mrs. Hudson personally attended. For the rest, with exceptions, a humbler servant was quite good enough. Many, indeed, had no attendance at all, after the outer door had been successfully negotiated; they climbed the seventeen steps alone, and knocked with their own knuckles. Where a visitor was familiar this was, of course, the rule. Hopkins, for instance, was allowed to go straight up, at any hour [1]; as was the portly Mycroft,[2] although he did not often attend upon his brother. In exceptional instances visitors were even allowed to enter the room in the absence of its tenants—a reckless business at best; but it is likely that by the case of Dr. Percy Trevelyan Mrs. Hudson's uncanny shrewdness in such decisions is attested. A 'pale, taper-faced man with sandy whiskers',[3] a haggard expression, and an unhealthy complexion, there can have been little enough about Trevelyan's outward appearance to recommend him. Holmes himself perhaps was hardly more apt at rapid diagnosis of a

---

[1] *Black Peter*, I, 698.
[2] *The Greek Interpreter*, I, 492.
[3] *The Resident Patient*, I 460.

stranger than Mrs. Hudson on her outer threshold. What he caught by observation and deduction may have been little more, in substance, than that revealed to her by intuition. It is proverbial that landladies are that way.

As somewhat qualifying this view of Martha Hudson—this suggestion of a certain snobbishness, which in no wise detracted from her fundamental kindliness and amiability—it may be ventured that she was a woman of curiosity; that is, she was a woman. There can be no doubt that she was a witness to some strange, impulsive entrances and some remarkable exits. That her extraordinary lodgers fascinated her, from the beginning of the long association to its end, is certain. It follows that where curiosity struggled with decorum, she would frequently indulge her curiosity. One fancies that she appeared at times with visitors of less importance than impatience, for no reason other than that their behaviour roused her interest. Did she ever listen outside the door? The suspicion is uncharitable and unworthy, and probably entirely justified. Just for an instant perhaps—a moment—after the barrier had been closed, to catch the opening lines of the drama? Perhaps to verify her own conjecture that *this* was a saddening case of lovers parted? And this natural curiosity would mildly operate with reference to the living-room. The very circumstance that her duties ended, for the most part, on the threshold, would make her the more eager to cross over. The room itself was somewhat of a mystery, chaotically filled as it was with the detective's souvenirs of crime and comfort. For one reason and another then, one thinks that Mrs. Hudson liked occasionally to get past the door, just to see what was going on. And while direct evidence is lacking, one thinks that she was not above a little innocent eaves-dropping.

They were all busy enough, heaven knows—maid, page, and landlady—showing people up, or simply answering the doorbell. The doctor's narratives are filled with the tramp of feet upon the stairs. And it is certain that the bell rang many times in the course of a single morning and afternoon. When Watson, waiting in the rooms for his friend's return from an investigation, tells us that ' every time a knock came to the door ' [1] he imagined it to be Holmes returning, he tells us also, by inference, that there were many knocks. Letters and cablegrams and newspapers were constantly arriving, particularly newspapers ; one gathers that every new edition found its way into the consulting-room. And coffee went up the

---

[1] *The Sign of Four*, II, 221.

stairs at almost mathematical intervals. No wonder there was a page-boy and a maid; and even so it is probable that Mrs. Hudson kept her flesh down somewhat with her constant climbing. 'From the years 1894 to 1901 inclusive, Mr. Sherlock Holmes was a very busy man,' [1] reports the doctor, in the opening sentence of his account of *The Solitary Cyclist*; but almost equally busy, we may be sure, was Mrs. Hudson and her little staff of servants.

It is not surprising that she went to bed about eleven; and she was quite definitely between the blankets on that stormy night in late November, 1894, when Hopkins' cabwheel grated against the kerb. It was Watson who had to let the inspector in. 'Run down, my dear fellow, and open the door,' said Sherlock Holmes, on that occasion, 'for all virtuous folk have been long in bed.' [2] That was the night they put up Hopkins on the sofa, in preparation for an early start, next morning, for Yoxley Old Place. There was a train at six from Charing Cross to Chatham, and the humane Holmes did not rouse his slumbering landlady.[3] They had coffee brewed on the detective's spirit-lamp.

[1] I, 639.
[2] *The Golden Pince-Nez*, I, 784.
[3] Ibid., 793.

Vincent Starrett

In Watson's sprightly narrative called *The Dying Detective* we have perhaps our clearest view of Mrs. Hudson, as she existed for the doctor. She was, he tells us in his first sentence, ' a long-suffering woman. Not only,' he continues, ' was her first-floor flat invaded at all hours by throngs of singular and often undesirable characters, but her remarkable lodger showed an eccentricity and irregularity in his life which must have sorely tried her patience. His incredible untidiness, his addiction to music at strange hours, his occasional revolver practice within doors, his weird and often malodorous scientific experiments, and the atmosphere of violence and danger which hung around him made him the very worst tenant in London.' [1]

One can hardly question the characterisation either of Holmes or Mrs. Hudson.

' On the other hand,' proceeds the doctor, as if it explained everything, ' his payments were princely. I have no doubt that the house might have been purchased at the price which Holmes paid for his rooms during the years that I was with him.' [2]

That is an assertion that opens up a subject with which we have no immediate concern—the

[1] I, 1000–1001.
[2] Ibid.

matter of Holmes' profits. As it relates to the rental paid by the detective, it is possibly more extravagant than significant. The impecunious Watson was no judge of what was princely. It is clear, however, that Holmes paid his landlady a decent sum of money, perhaps monthly, perhaps semi-monthly ; and it may be assumed that Watson thought the sum excessive. It would be idle to deny that the circumstance had some relation to the detective's continued tenancy of the rooms, and to Mrs. Hudson's regard for him. Certainly it is not the whole story, as Watson presently admits : ' The landlady stood in the deepest awe of him,' he tells us, ' and never dared to interfere with him, however outrageous his proceedings might seem ' ; *but* ' she was fond of him, too,' he confesses, ' for he had a remarkable gentleness and courtesy in his dealings with women.' [1]

And a little later : ' Knowing how genuine was her regard for him, I listened earnestly to her story when she came to my rooms in the second year of my married life and told me of the sad condition to which my poor friend was reduced.' [2]

Whatever Mrs. Hudson's awe of Sherlock Holmes, and no doubt it continued throughout

---

[1] *The Dying Detective*, I, 1001.
[2] Ibid.

the years, her sincere affection for him cannot be
questioned.   She believed him to be dying when
she rushed off to Watson on that November day
in 1888.   For three days she had seen him sinking,
while he refused to allow her to call in a doctor,
and her agitation was profound.   Watson was
horrified ; and they drove back together to the
rooms in Baker Street, Mrs. Hudson explaining
all the way.   ' You know how masterful he is,'
she said.   ' I didn't dare to disobey him.'   Yet,
' with your leave or without it, Mr. Holmes,' she
had told him at last, ' I am going for a doctor
this very hour.' [1]   It was not alone concern for a
profitable lodger that dictated her decision.
When Watson emerged from the sick-room she
' was waiting, trembling and weeping, in the
passage.' [2]   It is certain that she had been there
throughout the entire scene within.

   More than a year before, her affectionate concern for Holmes had been evident.   During the
excitements of the search for the Andaman
islander, she had been worried about the detective's health, and had even ventured—with a
doctor in the house—to prescribe ' a cooling
medicine.' [3]

[1] Ibid.
[2] Ibid., 1008.
[3] *The Sign of Four*, II, 218.

She would appear always to have been in
excellent health herself. Possibly Watson looked
after any small disorders that afflicted her while
he was a partner in the firm; but a landlady with a
cooling medicine in her cupboard would have her
own ways of looking after her health. What she
thought of Holmes' drug habits, until he aban-
doned them, is nowhere revealed; and the
strong probability is that she never suspected
them.

It is not strange that Holmes—in 1888—failed
to take her into his confidence in the little comedy
of *The Dying Detective*; in such dangerous matters
he played a lone hand, and very properly so. In
smaller deceptions he made flattering use of her,
as in the last scene of the adventure recorded as
The Naval Treaty, when she conspired with him
to serve up the missing papers under a breakfast
cover.[1] This innocent hoax tickled her im-
mensely, one likes to think. To have a hand in
any of her favourite lodger's enterprises must
always have pleased her. Her sense of humour
is not anywhere revealed as notable, however, and
it is likely that it did not often rise above com-
plicity in some such trickery as the episode of the
naval papers. Doubtless there were a number of
little pleasantries about the Persian slipper and

[1] I, 531.

the coal-scuttle, and doubtless they became a
bit familiar with repetition.

But the actual *adventures* of Mrs. Hudson were
for a number of years merely emotional states of
heart and mind occasioned by the rumblings of
the volcano on whose slopes she lived. They
were lightning flashes on a horizon that was
sometimes far off and sometimes close at hand.
They were sounds and apprehensions from the
living-room above ; swift pictures of detective
inspectors arriving in haste and prisoners departing under duress ; sinister figures on the doorstep. They were, in brief, the emanations from
that atmosphere of violence and danger which
made Mr. Sherlock Holmes, in Watson's considered phrase, ' the very worst tenant in
London.' [1] They were also, of course, the
adventures in anticipation, as it were, of the
innocent bystander, who—after all—is quite
likely to be hurt in any disturbance of which he
makes himself a part. Mrs. Hudson's adventures,
in the more literal meaning of the word, possibly
began with the determination of Professor
Moriarty to discourage the attentions of Mr.
Sherlock Holmes.

' No great harm was done' [2] the rooms in Baker

---

[1] *The Dying Detective*, I, 1001.
[2] *The Final Problem*, I, 547.

Street, we are told, by the fire started there by
Moriarty's agents, on a night in April, 1891; but
the shock to Mrs. Hudson must have been
considerable. We have no report of the actual
damage done, other than Holmes' laconic comment. The newspapers of the following day
carried an account of the outrage, from which it
would appear that Holmes derived his own
information. He was not in the rooms when
they were fired, and Watson was at that time
married and gone domestic ways. Unless she
had a crony in, Mrs. Hudson was alone with her
miniature staff of servants, and as such enterprises
as arson are carried out at secret hours, the
presumption is that they were all in bed. A pretty
disturbance they must have had; and Mrs.
Hudson undoubtedly sat up the rest of the night.

Thereafter came the tidings of Holmes' death
in Switzerland.

' It is with a heavy heart that I take up my pen
to write these last words in which I shall ever
record the singular gifts by which my friend Mr.
Sherlock Holmes was distinguished,' wrote Watson, in beginning his account of *The Final
Problem*.[1] His heart, we may be sure, was no
heavier than that of Martha Hudson. Only
Mycroft, of the intimate circle, knew that Holmes

[1] I, 536.

survived,[1] and what sentimental tale he told his brother's sorrowing housekeeper to account for keeping up the rooms in Baker Street we may only surmise. But it is quite possible that the admirable creature would have kept them up herself, merely for auld lang syne. One can imagine the tales with which she edified her cronies during the three years of the detective's absence. And her melancholy perambulations of the famous living-room, now at last wide open— like a museum—for her inspection.

But if she mourned for Holmes after the tidings of his death, the shock of his return produced an emotional disturbance even more intense; it threw her into violent hysterics.[2] Small wonder, of course : Watson himself, a little later, fainted for the first and last time in his life.[3] Resurrection must always, one fancies, occasion dramatics more spectacular than the more familiar pheno-menon of death. But she recovered from her shock when she realised that Holmes had need of her; and the adventure which followed was one of the high spots of Martha Hudson's life of service.

Holmes' plans had been quickly made. The

[1] *The Empty House*, I, 568.
[2] Ibid., 569.
[3] Ibid., 564.

remaining members of the gang, whose leader lay dead beneath the Reichenbach, knew that he had returned. Unknown to Mrs. Hudson, although probably suspected by brother Mycroft, they had watched the rooms with unceasing hatred, after his disappearance, knowing that some day he would return.[1] Incidentally, it is obvious that more of them escaped the police net than Scotland Yard admitted in its telegram to Holmes in Switzerland.[2]

In the capture of the desperate Colonel Sebastian Moran, Moriarty's underling, Mrs. Hudson played her part with intelligence and courage. Eight times in the course of two hours, while Holmes and Watson waited in the empty house across the way, the silhouetted shadow of the detective's bust changed its shape upon the blind, as Martha Hudson, on her hands and knees, operated the facsimile in the lighted living-room.[3] Then the Colonel's bullet shattered the window-glass, passed accurately through the waxen skull, and flattened against the opposite wall. Mrs. Hudson picked it from the carpet as coolly as she would have lifted a penny.[4]

[1] *The Empty House*, I, 572.
[2] *The Final Problem*, I, 550; cp. *The Empty House*, I, 568–569.
[3] *The Empty House*, I, 574.
[4] Ibid., 579.

Vincent Starrett

Holmes was obliged to her for her assistance, and told her so—a trifle abruptly, it would appear from Watson's record of the scene,[1] but it was sufficient for Mrs. Hudson. A laconic word of praise from Sherlock Holmes went a long way with those who served him. She was a bit distressed, however, by the ruin wrought by the Colonel's marksmanship: 'I'm afraid it has spoiled your beautiful bust,'[2] she told the detective, a little later, handing him the bullet.

The place had been put in order during Holmes' absence; his supposed death had furnished an opportunity for straightening up that Mrs. Hudson, for all her grief, had not failed to remark. 'Our old chambers,' wrote Watson, in *The Empty House,* 'had been left unchanged, through the supervision of Mycroft Holmes and the immediate care of Mrs. Hudson. As I entered I saw, it is true, an unwonted tidiness, but the old landmarks were all in their places. There were the chemical corner and the acid-stained deal-top table. There upon a shelf was the row of formidable scrap-books and books of reference which many of our fellow-citizens would have been so glad to burn. The diagrams, the violin-case, and the pipe-rack—even the Persian slipper

[1] Ibid.
[2] Ibid.

which contained the tobacco—all met my eye as I glanced round me.' [1]

A happy homecoming, one must believe, for all of them. Thereafter, too, the relationship must have been somewhat closer. Holmes was never at any time demonstrative, even in his relations with Watson; and Mrs. Hudson was clearly a woman who knew her place and was careful to occupy it: but it is impossible not to believe that a new warmth entered the situation after the detective's return from the dead. Holmes' proverbial distrust of the sex [2] was surely qualified, after the adventure of *The Empty House*, by a distinguished exception made in favour of Mrs. Hudson. Later events, indeed, were to prove that he did hold both her courage and intelligence in the highest respect; so much so that, in an hour of his own and his country's need, it was of Martha Hudson that he thought and to Martha Hudson that he turned for assistance.

Meanwhile, the old connections had been restored. In Baker Street, again, all was as it had been and as it ever shall be. Watson, whose wife had died in the detective's absence,[3] was back

[1] *The Empty House*, I, 579.
[2] *The Dying Detective*, I, 1001.
[3] *The Empty House*, I, 569.

once more in his old room, and events were shaping toward the adventures of *The Second Stain* and *The Golden Pince-Nez* : episodes dated in the last quarter of that memorable year 1894.

The years that followed were to bring to Holmes, and vicariously to Mrs. Hudson, some of the most surprising of his many experiences. Patrick Cairns, the murderer of 'Black Peter' Carey, was to be captured in the rooms in Baker Street, after a struggle that to Mrs. Hudson must have been reminiscent of that which preceded the taking of Jefferson Hope.[1] The wild-eyed and unhappy John Hector McFarlane was to clatter up the stairs with every evidence of madness [2]; the portly Mycroft was to drive through yellow fog to his brother's doorstep, with tidings of sensational import [3]; and Dr. Thorneycroft Huxtable, M.A., Ph.D., was to crash prostrate and insensible upon the bearskin rug.[4] Illustrious clients in number were to cross the threshold of the consulting-room,[5] and Holmes was to refuse a knighthood for services that never have been revealed.[6] Watson, good fellow, was to take

[1] *Black Peter*, I, 715.
[2] *The Norwood Builder*, I, 584.
[3] *The Bruce-Partington Plans*, I, 968 ff.
[4] *The Priory School*, I, 661.
[5] *Black Peter*, I, 696 ; *The Illustrious Client*, I, 1090.
[6] *The Three Garridebs*, I, 1196.

another wife,[1] though whose he took is still a
matter much debated. Throughout all these
scenes of triumph and disorder moved Martha
Hudson on her daily round. Her figure, we may
assume, grew thicker as the years went past, and
possibly she climbed the stairs less often than had
been her practice in earlier days. A hired cook,
as we have seen, had for some years relieved her
of the task of cooking. There was, one thinks,
more leisure on her hands. It would be satisfying
to know what use she made of it.

It has always been a minor mystery what
relaxations she favoured in her spare time,
assuming that she had time to spare. There were
her cronies, to be sure, but cinemas had not yet
been invented. One fancies that she took to
patience, and later on—as we shall see—to
knitting. When Holmes played upon his violin,
we may be sure she sat and listened, rapt by the
strains that also soothed and charmed the sentimental doctor. Madame Tussaud's was close at
hand, and it is likely that its Chamber of Horrors
displayed a murderer or two of Holmes' plucking.
One sees her there on rainy afternoons, perhaps
renewing old acquaintances.

What she thought of Watson's marriages is not
included in the record. That she was fond of

[1] *The Blanched Soldier*, I, 1118.

Mary Morstan can easily be imagined; and it may be that she wondered why the doctor, after his wife's death, did not at once return to Baker Street. She was not the sort, however, to venture comment on a delicate subject. Whomever Watson married, in 1902 or 1903, we may be certain that she offered her congratulations with good humour and sincerity. But Holmes' refusal of a knighthood must have tried her patience sorely.

In the matter of Sherlock Holmes' disguises, over the years of the relationship, it would be interesting to know what passed between them. There was a streak of mischief in the detective; it is impossible not to believe that he tried them out upon her, with amusing results. She had sharp eyes, and it may be assumed that if he passed their scrutiny unrecognised, he was content that others too would be deluded. It is notorious that he fooled Watson and Athelney Jones without half trying [1]; but in Mrs. Hudson he must have recognised an intelligence of a different order. It is likely that sometimes she dismayed him. Like the landlady in Aristophanes, she may have asked, upon occasion: 'Did you expect I would not know you again because you had buskins on?' Or words to that

[1] *The Sign of Four*, II, 223–225.

effect. With his more usual mummery she was, of course, familiar, and the spectacle of an asthmatic seafaring gentleman creeping up the stairs,[1] believing himself unknown, just conceivably may have caused her to stand below and giggle.

Once in the early days Holmes called her Turner—Mrs. Turner. So Watson, at any rate, sets forth in *A Scandal in Bohemia*. ' When Mrs. Turner has brought in the tray I will make it clear to you,' [2] said the detective, as alleged by Watson ; meaning that he would make clear what service he demanded of the doctor. The remark has been anything but clear to students of the record. That Holmes actually made it may be doubted ; it is too obviously the sort of error Watson would commit in the throes of composition. No doubt, at the moment of writing, a patient named Turner was waiting in his consulting-room—was in some fashion, anyway, upon his mind. The story was written by the doctor in 1891,[3] after the supposed death of Holmes in Switzerland, about an adventure dated in 1888 ; that is, it was written during the early weeks of his mourning for his friend, at a time when he was distraught.

[1] Ibid., 223 ; *Black Peter*, I, 697.
[2] I, 19.
[3] It appeared in the *Strand Magazine* for July, 1891.

It is not for a moment to be supposed that Watson forgot the name of his old landlady, but it *is* a bit to his discredit, one thinks, that not once during the three years of Holmes' absence did he call upon her.

So they lived in Baker Street, and so always shall they live ; the detective and the doctor and, below stairs, the humble and loyal housekeeper whose happiness it was to serve them. The actual term of the detective's tenancy was from February, 1881,[1] until late in 1903—more probably until the early months of 1904. The date of Holmes' retirement from practice is not set forth by Watson ; but in September, 1903, he was still actively engaged on the extraordinary adventure of *The Creeping Man*,[2] and by December, 1904,[3] he had definitely retired to bee-keeping on the Sussex Downs. The hegira from London occurred some time in the months between, and the probabilities are perhaps in favour of a removal during the spring months of the latter year.

Thus ended the long Baker Street career of Mr.

[1] The *Study in Scarlet* was called to his attention on March 4th ; during the ' first week or so ' (II, 18) there had been no callers.

[2] I, 1244.

[3] *The Second Stain*, I, 859.   Published in the *Strand Magazine*, December, 1904.

Sherlock Holmes, consulting specialist in crime ; and with it, one thinks, Mrs. Hudson's tenancy of the premises made famous by her remarkable lodger. Whether she owned the building or merely herself rented it from another, is not clear ; but—although it is nowhere explicitly asserted—there can be no reasonable doubt that she retired with Holmes to Sussex ; if not at once, then later. Writing, in his retirement, of the curious mystery of *The Lion's Mane*, it is Holmes himself who furnishes the clue. ' My house is lonely,' he tells us. ' I, my old house-keeper, and my bees have the estate all to ourselves.' [1] This was in 1926, in which year the detective published the reminiscence.[2] He was writing, however, of an adventure that occurred in 1907, and even then Mrs. Hudson was with him. It was she who first heard of the curious incident of Fitzroy McPherson's dog,[3] and mentioned it to Holmes—although he did not encourage gossip of the countryside.

Thereafter the record of her service is a blank until the second day of August, 1914—' the most terrible August in the history of the world.' [4] On that evening two famous Germans stood upon

[1] I, 1267.
[2] In the *Strand Magazine*, December, 1926.
[3] *The Lion's Mane*, I, 1278.
[4] *His Last Bow*, I, 1068.

the terrace of a house near Harwich. ' Only one
window showed a light behind them ; in it there
stood a lamp, and beside it, seated at a table, was
a dear old ruddy-faced woman in a country cap.
She was bending over her knitting and stopping
occasionally to stroke a large black cat upon a
stool beside her.' [1] With her self-absorption
and ' general air of comfortable somnolence,' [2]
thought one of the Germans, she might have
personified Britannia herself.

'Who is that ? ' asked Von Herling, the
secretary of legation ; and Von Bork replied :
' That is Martha, the only servant I have left.' [3]

She looked with apprehension at the figure on
the sofa, a little later, when Von Bork lay trussed
and helpless, and seemed distressed that it was
she who had brought him to that pass. ' According to his lights,' she said, he had been a kindly
master.[4] For two years she had served him
faithfully, by Holmes' order, and at length she
had betrayed him—the master spy of Germany.
The dousing of her lamp had been the signal for
the detective's entrance. It was Martha Hudson's
last adventure, as far as it is possible for research
to discover. In all things she had played her part

[1] *His Last Bow*, I, 1074.
[2] Ibid.
[3] Ibid.
[4] Ibid., 1080.

to admiration, Holmes told the doctor when he
came upon the scene : ' I got her the situation
when first I took the matter up.'[1] Once more
in the history of the world, a woman's wit had
saved a mighty nation from disaster.

She was to report to Holmes upon the morrow
at Claridge's Hotel[2]; and there can be no
question that they returned, in time, to their
cottage on the Sussex Downs. It is a pleasant
place in which, with Sherlock Holmes, she now
passes her declining years ; and they are eighty,
each of them, if they are a day.[3] Mrs. Hudson,
in all likelihood, is even older. Certainly she was
no younger than Holmes when he became her
lodger. Her ' stately tread,'[4] in 1881 would
suggest at least a woman in her prime. Is it
possible that she is verging on her first century ?

But it is proverbial that landladies never die.

' My villa,' wrote Holmes, in 1926, ' is situated
upon the southern slope of the Downs, command-
ing a great view of the Channel. At this point
the coast-line is entirely of chalk cliffs, which can
only be descended by a single, long, tortuous
path, which is steep and slippery. At the bottom

[1] Ibid.
[2] Ibid., 1081.
[3] Sherlock Holmes is believed to have been born in
1854.
[4] *A Study in Scarlet*, II, 50.

of the path lie a hundred yards of pebbles and shingle, even when the tide is at full. Here and there, however, there are curves and hollows which make splendid swimming-pools filled afresh with each flow.' [1] It is a description richly filled with pictorial suggestion, and the possibilities turn one a little giddy. The wonder is that they do not break their necks.

In the evenings, if he still lives, Harold Stackhurst sometimes drops in for a chat [2] and, probably, a cup of Mrs. Hudson's tea. We may imagine that the conversation runs a bit to bees and rheumatism, then swings to days and nights in Baker Street. Lucky Harold Stackhurst! Only occasionally does Watson visit them, [3] which is perhaps unfortunate for the record. But Holmes, presumably, still adds a chapter, now and then, to that text-book which was to be the fruit of his declining years—which was to ' focus the whole art of detection ' into a single volume. [4] The long winter evenings, when the bees and Mrs. Hudson have been sent to bed, should be an admirable time for literary composition.

[1] *The Lion's Mane*, I, 1267.
[2] Ibid.
[3] Ibid., 1266.
[4] *The Abbey Grange*, I, 834.

The Mystery of Mycroft

RONALD A. KNOX

I could not have believed that you would have descended to this. You have made inquiries into the history of my unhappy brother.

THE SIGN OF FOUR

THE MYSTERY OF MYCROFT

IT is an ignominious destiny to be known as the brother of an immortal. If John Keats had little porridge or none, what ambrosia, what honeydew, had George? How humiliating, to re-introduce yourself to a half-witted neighbour at dinner, with 'No, no, *William* Rossetti, madam,' or 'Adolphus Trollope, not Anthony, I'm afraid!' Something, doubtless, of this mortification fell to the lot of Mycroft Holmes, and is reflected in his first greeting when he met Watson, 'I hear of Sherlock everywhere since you became his chronicler.'[1] He consoled himself, however, with the familiar refuge of the obscure—he had the power to become great, he told himself, but lacked the taste for it. 'Sherlock has all the energy of the family.'[2] Nor, in his case, was the boast a vain one; we have the testimony of his brother to that effect, and what a brother! One who was never deceived by false appearances, nor allowed himself, like the logician he was, to mis-state facts through modesty.

[1] *The Greek Interpreter*, I, 481.
[2] Ibid., 490.

Ronald A. Knox

'When I say, therefore, that Mycroft has better powers of observation than I, you may take it that I am speaking the exact and literal truth.' [1] We might have been able to form a different estimate of the part he played in the history of his family if we lacked this assurance. But the thing is certain; there were no flies on Mycroft Holmes, even when he was examined under the lens of Sherlock.

Did space permit, we could while away several paragraphs by reconstructing, from scattered indications, the atmosphere of their common boyhood. It will have been passed, I fancy, in the country; for they came of a family of squires,[2] and Mycroft, Londoner as he was in his habits, found no difficulty in turning to and driving a brougham [3]: skilfully, too, or it would hardly have been possible for him, even in those days, to 'dash away' from the midst of the traffic outside Victoria Station.[4] For the rest, they must have shared the simple pleasures of a country upbringing, made more poignant to them by that remarkable gift of observation which they shared. Mycroft, the senior by seven years, will have exploded the myth of Santa Claus while

[1] Ibid., 479.
[2] Ibid., I, 478.
[3] *The Final Problem*, I, 548.
[4] Ibid., 546.

Sherlock was still puling in the cradle; and in a
hundred other ways Sherlock will have been
disabused, from the first, of illusion. Once
trousered, he will have taken the lead in their
sports, merely from his native energy. You
picture Mycroft sprawling on a hearth-rug and
prophesying the whereabouts of the birds' nests
he was too indolent to take; deducing what
village boys, by what devious routes, had been
responsible for depredations on the orchard, and
fagging Sherlock to get out of bed and catch them
red-handed. A call on the Holmes family must
have been an unnerving business; you could be
sure that you would be turned inside out the
moment you had left. 'Mummy,' little Sherlock
would say, 'Who was that man who came to
luncheon? I mean the victim of chronic
alcoholism with the dirty finger-nails? I could
see, of course, that he nas trouble with his wife,
and that his gas-bill for last quarter remains un-
paid; that he is thriftless, absent-minded, and
Eurasian by descent; but I couldn't quite make
out whether he was a company-promoter or just
a common blackmailer?' Then from the hearth-
rug: 'Don't make such an unnecessary ass of
yourself, you blighter; do you mean to say you
can't tell a publisher from the way he licks his
finger before turning over a page of manuscript?'

' My dears,' Mrs. Holmes would expostulate, crushing down a Sempronia's pride in the interests of manners, ' you really must not say such things.'

They were North-country folk, I take it ; the Southern counties are fairly well covered by Watson's reminiscences, and in no instance does his friend betray familiarity with, or enthusiasm over, the local scenery. I seem to see their home as a Vicarage, decently but not abundantly provided with material comforts. Their father's theological views cannot be accurately determined, in the absence of any evidence whether William or Thomas Sherlock was the detective's eponym. The works of either divine must have made dry reading for Sunday afternoons, but they will have had their formative influence ; one may attribute a certain fondness for moralising to this source. As for Mycroft, it might easily be supposed at first sight that his christening reflected the tastes of a cricket fan. But he was born, if Mr. Bell's calculation is right, in 1847, and at that date the future bowler for Derbyshire had only attained his sixth year. Probably, then, Mycroft was a family name ; and one may even conjecture that it was bestowed on the condition, or in the hope, of a legacy from some relative. The hope seems in any case to have been frustrated. The early struggles of the detective suggest that he had no private means; and when he tells Watson that his brother 'draws four hundred and fifty pounds a year'[1] he gives no hint of an independent source of income.

Was Mycroft a senior or a junior clerk? That he should be in receipt of £450 a year at the age of forty-eight is a circumstance which throws no light on the question. On the whole, it seems probable that he was a senior clerk who had entered the service by some back-door after experience elsewhere. On the intervening period Watson is silent; and his silence is the reflection of Sherlock's. To this problem we must now address ourselves: Why was it that Holmes, during nearly ten years of their intimacy, made no allusion to a brother who was living a few streets away? It was not that the relations between the two brothers were strained, or their communication intermittent: 'Again and again I have taken a problem to him.'[2] 'Some of my most interesting cases have come to me in this way through Mycroft.'[3] It is true Mycroft never came to Baker Street except once before the

[1] *The Bruce-Partington Plans*, I, 970.
[2] *The Greek Interpreter*, I, 479.
[3] Ibid., 491.

Bruce-Partington case,[1] and that must have been
over the affair of the Greek Interpreter,[2] so there
was no reason why Watson should actually have
encountered him, although, as we know, it was
part of Watson's duty to admit visitors when
Mrs. Hudson had gone to bed.[3]   But it is
incredible that Holmes should have made no
mention of a surviving member of his family, and
one who lived so close, if there had been no
reason behind his silence.   Watson, to be sure,
only once alludes to his own brother, but with
cause ; for that brother had been a drunkard,[4]
and it is not unlikely that the taint was hereditary.[5]

The mystery is only deepened by the fact that
Sherlock, on his own admission, did not tell
Watson the whole truth about his brother, even
when he divulged the secret of that brother's
existence.   At the time of the story of *The Greek
Interpreter*, Watson was given to understand that
Mycroft held ' some small office under the British
Government.'[6]   It is only in the story of *The
Bruce-Partington Plans* that he is introduced to the
true facts ; Mycroft holds a position so important

[1] I, 969.
[2] I, 492.
[3] *The Golden Pince-Nez*, I, 784.
[4] *The Sign of Four*, II, 150.
[5] Ibid., 143, 162, 174.
[6] *The Bruce-Partington Plans*, I, 970.

that ' occasionally he *is* the British Government.' [1]
And what explanation does the detective give of
his former evasiveness ? ' I did not know you
quite so well in those days.' [2] It is safe to say
that the explanation is one which would have
taken in nobody except Watson. Holmes is
speaking in the winter of 1895 ; he is speaking
about the summer of 1890. In 1890 the little
community of Baker Street had already been in
existence for nine years. During that period we
have no record of a single occasion when Watson
was so much as sent out of the room, even when
the secrets of royalty were being discussed.[3] Can
we really believe that Holmes felt, so late in their
acquaintance, any difficulty in reading his friend's
character ? Did Sherlock ? If so, the less
Sherlock he. Only one explanation is really
tenable ; he told Watson as little as possible
about Mycroft in 1890 because there was a secret
in Mycroft's life which must at all costs be hushed
up.

Why then, it will be asked, did Holmes mention
his brother at all ? Did the reference fall from his
lips by accident ? Hardly ; it was under no stress
of sudden emotion.[4] A better explanation lies

[1] Ibid., I, 970.
[2] Loc. cit.
[3] E.g., *A Scandal in Bohemia*, I, 9.
[4] *The Greek Interpreter*, I, 478.

ready to hand; Holmes deliberately mentioned his brother, deliberately effected an introduction, because his brother was to play an important *role* in the final phases of his struggle with Moriarty. Moriarty, indeed, was not aware that a crisis was impending until January of 1891, some five or six months later.[1] But Holmes, we know, had ' had it in ' for Moriarty since 1889 at the latest.[2] He knew that the encounter would be full of danger for himself; he might want to use Mycroft as his protector,[3] his coachman,[4] his supposed executor [5] and actual confidant.[6] Evidently it was best that Watson and Mycroft should meet, and meet soon. It was with full deliberation that Holmes walked his friend round to the Diogenes Club on that summer evening of 1890.

Even so, Watson was told little, and that little was misleading. He must not be led on to grow inquisitive about Mycroft, because there was that in Mycroft's record which did not bear looking into. What was it? To get at some inkling of the truth it is necessary to examine very carefully the story of *The Greek Interpreter*.

[1] *The Final Problem*, I, 542.
[2] *The Valley of Fear*, II, 640.
[3] *The Final Problem*, I, 544.
[4] Ibid., 548.
[5] Ibid., 556.
[6] *The Empty House*, I, 568.

Quite casually, in the strangers' room of the Diogenes Club, Mycroft remembers that a Greek, who lodges in the rooms above him, has had a curious experience. The Greek is brought over, and explains how, two nights before, he was decoyed into a cab and taken off to an unknown house in the suburbs, where he acted as interpreter in an interview between another Greek (called Kratides) and two obvious crooks, who wanted him to sign away his property under compulsion of hunger. The police have heard the story, but appear to give it no credit; the Greek Legation knows nothing; Mycroft has put an advertisement in the papers advertising for the whereabouts of Sophy Kratides, the prisoner's sister. Sherlock and Watson go back to Baker Street, sending some telegrams on the way, one of which will evidently have been addressed to the Athens police. Arriving at 221B, they find that Mycroft is there ahead of them, having arrived in a cab. He has had an answer to his advertisement from Mr. J. Davenport, who writes from Lower Brixton. (The name of the paper in which he had seen it is not mentioned, but I have an instinct that it was the *Daily Telegraph*.) Mycroft proposes a journey to Lower Brixton; Sherlock, better advised, is for getting a police warrant and searching The Myrtles, Beckenham, at which address (*teste* Davenport) Sophy Kratides is residing.

On their way to Scotland Yard they call to pick up Mr. Melas the interpreter, and find that he has once more been decoyed away by one of the villains. Precious time is wasted in getting the proper legal proceedings put through at the Yard; then they make for Beckenham by train, force an entrance into The Myrtles, and find that its occupants have flown. But the two Greeks, Melas and Kratides, have been left in an upper room, where, tied hand and foot, they are being slowly suffocated with charcoal. Kratides is too far gone for help; Melas recovers, and explains all he knows of the situation. It appears, from J. Davenport's account, that Sophy Kratides has married Latimer, one of the two villains, against the advice of her friends, and that her brother came over to attempt her rescue. ' Months afterwards a curious newspaper cutting reached us from Buda-Pesth,' describing the death of two English travellers by stabbing; Holmes conjectures that this was Sophy Kratides' vengeance on the murderers of her brother.

I have no doubt that Watson faithfully reported the facts as the facts were known to him; that confidence is basic to all our study of Holmes literature. But it does not follow that he saw all that was going on. I will invite my readers to consider a number of curious anomalies about the story given above, and to ask themselves whether these cannot be easily resolved if we entertain a suspicion Watson never entertained— that Mycroft was no stranger to the villains of the story, Latimer and Kemp, and was indeed *working in their interest all through.*

(i.) It is a coincidence, surely, that Mr. Melas, whose services were so necessary to Latimer and Kemp, should actually have been lodging in the same house as the brother of the great detective who was to deal with the mystery. Crime does not, in real life, follow detectives about. The coincidence disappears, if we suppose that Mycroft was the ally, whereas Melas had somehow incurred the enmity, of Kemp and Latimer. Mycroft's landlady, herself attached to the gang, had offered exceptionally cheap terms, and so lured the esurient Greek into her top attic. He is now in his enemies' power. A host of minor difficulties are thus settled ; as, how it is conceivable that Kemp and Kratides should not have had enough French to carry on their extremely staccato dialogue in that tongue ; or why it was that Kemp could threaten the interpreter with discovery if he should mention what he had seen. ' We shall know if you speak of this. We have

our own means of information.' [1] What means
of information could two gentlemen in Beckenham have about the behaviour of a Greek
Interpreter living in Pall Mall, *unless he were
living under the same roof as their accomplice*?

(ii.) Why was not Sherlock told earlier? The
case was clearly urgent; here you had a man
starving; Mycroft, for all his indolence, would
surely have called in his brother if he had not
been squared in the interests of the villains. On
the other hand, the police had been informed, on
Tuesday morning, one supposes; would not
they have called Baker Street into consultation?
The answer is, clearly, that they did; that
Sherlock had already heard Melas' story in out-
line from Lestrade; that he went to the Diogenes
Club in order to get fuller information; and that
Mycroft, guessing his errand, anticipated him by
alluding to the incident of his own accord.

(iii.) In the meantime, what had Mycroft done?
What any fool would have had the sense to avoid
doing, you would have thought; he had adver-
tised in all the morning papers for the whereabouts of Sophy Kratides. Mycroft was no fool;
he knew exactly what he was doing. He was in
effect sending a signal to his accomplices in
Beckenham to say, ' Your secret is out, and the

[1] I, 489.

police are already on your track. Charcoal for two.' It is ridiculous to suggest that advertising was the only possible resource. As Sherlock pointed out, the Athens police might have been notified. Enquiries might have been made around Wandsworth Common for information about the appearance there early on Tuesday morning of a gentleman's brougham, with a horse in it that had covered thirty miles since nightfall. Again, if Melas had been pressed about the length of the ' interminable drive ' which ended at midnight on Wandsworth Common, it would have been easy to construct a triangle showing the Beckenham district and the Ealing district as strict alternatives ; neither of these was then seriously overgrown with houses, and a local chemist would have remembered the little giggling gentleman to whom he sold an unusual quantity of sticking-plaster. The only fatal thing was to advertise, and Mycroft did it.

(iv.) Why did Mycroft, on receiving a letter from J. Davenport, immediately take a cab and visit, for the first time in his life, Sherlock's rooms ? Why, if he was in a cab, did he not pick up Melas on his way ? The answer is clear—he knew that Kemp was coming, in a few minutes, to kidnap Melas for the second time from the lodgings in Pall Mall. To be there, or even to be at the Diogenes Club, just round the corner, might conceivably implicate him, Mycroft. An alibi was indicated : what better alibi than to take a cab, and rejoin his brother in Baker Street ?

(v.) Why did he propose a visit to J. Davenport at Brixton, when the Beckenham address was already known, and it was obviously important to interfere as soon as possible in that quarter ? The only reasonable answer is that he wanted to waste time, so that the unfortunate Melas might be thoroughly overcome by the charcoal fumes before help arrived. His suggestion was over-ruled ; it awoke, naturally, no suspicion in the breast of a Watson ; but can we say the same about Sherlock ? None were expressed ; but, as we shall see later, it is probable that Sherlock knew a good deal about his brother's nefarious associations, and was at pains to conceal his knowledge. What seems certain, at the present stage in our argument, is that Mycroft was a man who did not shrink from aiding and abetting murder.

On the other hand, it can hardly be supposed that a man of his attainments would have leagued himself with a couple of garrotters like Latimer and Kemp with any good will. The association can only be explained if we conjecture that both he and they were part of a greater organisation.

Enough said, for every student of Holmes literature ; the next word that leaps to the mind is MORIARTY. In suggesting that Mycroft was, at this period of his life, in the service and in the pay of the ex-Professor I shall, I know, awake a certain amount of incredulity. But we must face the facts ; 'when you have eliminated the impossible'—it is Sherlock's own maxim— 'whatever remains, however improbable, must be the truth.' It is not difficult to reconstruct the situation. The Holmes family lose, we know not how, what money they had. Mycroft gets an appointment, somehow, which involves auditing the books in some of the Government departments [1] ; it is probable enough that even this post, bestowed on him in view of his ' extraordinary faculty for figures,' was obtained through the influence of one who had formerly been a professor of mathematics. In any case, it is doubtful whether Mycroft was at this time anything more than a junior clerk ; how was he to recruit his finances so as to live the life he loved, alternating between the Diogenes Club and his lodgings, surely not inexpensive, in Pall Mall ? The answer was found to the problem when he lent his talents to ' the Napoleon of crime.' It suited Moriarty's book to have an eye kept on the

[1] *The Greek Interpreter*, I, 480.

ledgers of the Civil Service. But there was more to it than that ; Mycroft, as we discover later on, had a genius for co-ordination ; ' all other men are specialists, but his specialism is omniscience.' [1] Moriarty was engaged in organising the criminal activities of London, with their inevitable overlapping, frictions, clashes of interest ; in such work Mycroft would be invaluable to him.

But this would not suffice for the ambitions of Sherlock's brother. His peculiar position gave him the opportunity of acquiring favour, and to some extent financial help, by divulging Moriarty's secrets to Sherlock. It is easy to understand that some of his ' most interesting cases ' came to him through Mycroft, and that Mycroft was able to supply his brother, perplexed over a difficult problem, with ' an explanation which was afterwards proved to be the correct one.' Although the thing cannot be proved, I am strongly of the opinion that Mycroft was in fact the ' Fred Porlock ' who acted as his brother's informer in *The Valley of Fear*. Sherlock— Porlock ; there is a subconscious reminiscence in the choice of an *alias* which suggests a family connection. And who more likely than Mycroft, with his tidy and orderly brain, his great capacity

[1] *The Bruce-Partington Plans*, I, 970.

for storing facts,[1] to use *Whitaker's Almanack* as
the basis of a cipher message?

There, then, you have Mycroft; a man playing
a delicate part in an irreconcilable duel between
his brother on the one hand, and a super-criminal
on the other; a man open, certainly, to criticism,
but not devoid of generous qualities. We have
now to consider the attitude he adopts at the
crucial moment of *The Final Problem*. On the
one side, it is clear that information leaked from
Holmes' camp into that of his adversary. ' If I
could have done this without the knowledge of
Professor Moriarty, all would have been well.
But he was too wily for that. He saw every step
which I took to draw my toils round him.' [2] On
the other hand, it is clear that Mycroft would not
lend himself to any machinations against his
brother's life which might involve family un-
pleasantness. Mycroft's rooms in Pall Mall are
' home,' so to speak, in the great game between
the two protagonists; it is there that Sherlock
takes refuge after he has nearly been run over by
a van and nearly been killed by a falling brick on
a single morning.[3] He was no longer safe when
he had left; a rough with a bludgeon attacked

---

[1] Loc. cit.
[2] *The Final Problem*, I, 541.
[3] Ibid., 544.

him on his way round to Watson's house. There (though only when he left by way of the back garden) the scent cooled; Moriarty contented himself with setting fire to 221B Baker Street, while Sherlock roamed the streets unobserved. Everything depended on the next day, and on Watson's co-operation. We must be pardoned for recalling to the reader's mind the exact arrangements made for the flight to the Continent.

Watson was to send his luggage to Victoria overnight; was to hail a hansom cab next morning, neither the first nor the second which presented itself; to jump into this, and hand the driver a slip of paper telling him to make for the Strand end of the Lowther Arcade; arrived there, he was to bolt down the Arcade, and get into a private carriage which would take him straight to his destination. Now, we have Watson's own word for it that he carried out this programme, even to the extent of jumping into a hansom cab, a considerable feat. Watson was reckoned fleet of foot,[1] and he must have made good running down the Arcade; successful pursuit would be impossible, considering the difficulty of watching your man and dodging at top speed through a crowd at the same moment. Yet Moriarty

[1] *The Hound of the Baskervilles*, II, 435.

charged into Victoria Station when the boat-train had only just begun to move—so close was he on the track of his victim. How do we explain his presence? Sherlock is content to conjecture, 'They have evidently taken the precaution of watching you [Watson] . . . and this is what has brought Moriarty to Victoria.'[1] The theory, as we have seen, is inadmissible; and Holmes must have known that it was inadmissible. He produced it, only in order to screen his brother by concealing the real solution. He was nearly caught at Victoria because he had been betrayed by Mycroft.

It was Mycroft, as we know, who was driving the carriage that stood at the further end of the Lowther Arcade.[2] Evidently he had his orders from Sherlock; without a word spoken, he drives to Victoria. Why, then, was Moriarty not waiting at Victoria to intercept his victim? If Mycroft knew, Moriarty knew. True enough, but Moriarty's victim was Holmes, not Watson. And Moriarty naturally assumed that Watson's expedition was merely a piece of bluff; Sherlock would send Watson off by the boat-train to Dover, and would himself make for Southampton *via* Waterloo. Or would he play a game of

[1] *The Final Problem*, I, 548.
[2] Loc. cit.

double bluff, and set out with Watson after all ?
Moriarty, in his uncertainty, was forced to play
a waiting game ; he lay hidden somewhere handy,
probably at Mycroft's rooms in Pall Mall.
Mycroft deposited Watson at Victoria, and
' dashed away,' but not before he had caught
sight of an aged Italian priest who was, recognis-
ably to the eyes of a brother, Sherlock in make-up.
He drove off at full speed to pick up Moriarty,
with the assurance that Sherlock was indeed *en
route* for Dover. Having picked up Moriarty,
did he drive him at full speed, or only pretend to
drive him at full speed, back to Victoria ? We
shall never know ; it is an interesting psychological speculation. Anyhow, whether Mycroft
pulled the horse, or was held up by a genuine
traffic-block, the plan just miscarried ; the boat-
train slid out, leaving Moriarty to blaspheme on
the main platform.

We might have hoped that the break-up of the
gang, and Moriarty's own death on the Reichenbach, would have effected a change of heart in
Mycroft, and that he would have enrolled himself, thenceforward, under the banners of civilisa-
tion. But it is painfully evident that Colonel
Moran, the surviving leader of the forlorn hope,
exercised a strong influence over our hero, if
only by way of blackmail. Sherlock himself

explains that when the rest of the world thought him dead, he had only one confidant, his brother.[1] Mycroft kept the secret from Watson; unfortunately he did not observe a similar reticence in other directions. When Sherlock makes himself known to Watson on his return, he states expressly that he has only arrived in London from the Continent that day.[2] Yet that same evening Colonel Moran is stalking 221B with an airgun. How are we to explain the accuracy of his information? Sherlock, as usual, gives us, not the true explanation, but one which will do for Watson. Moriarty's gang, those of them who were left, knew that he was alive; 'sooner or later they believed that I should come back to my rooms. They watched them continuously, and this morning they saw me arrive.' [3] *Credat Judæus Apella*; you do not really watch a house, on the chance of its being revisited, for three years on end. No, Colonel Moran's information will have come, as usual, from Mycroft; Sherlock, as usual, conceals the equivocal part his brother has been playing in the drama, and fobs off his credulous biographer with a manifest lie.

To do Mycroft justice, it should be remarked

[1] *The Empty House*, I, 568.
[2] Ibid., 569.
[3] Ibid., I, 572.

that in this matter he had probably the intention of betraying, not his brother, but Colonel Moran. The bust of Sherlock, carefully executed by M. Meunier, of Grenoble, can hardly have reached Baker Street without Mycroft's knowledge ; and he was probably aware, therefore, that in divulging the news of Sherlock's return he was in effect baiting a trap. All the same, it is repellent to our better instincts to find Mycroft still the trusted ally of a Colonel Moran, when the Moriarty gang had been scattered to the winds. Some people never seem to know when they are beaten.

How much did Sherlock know, how much did he suspect, of his brother's duplicities all through ? And what use did he make of his knowledge ? We have no exact information on the point ; but it seems likely that Moriarty lost more than he gained by the employment of such an agent. He did not know that he was being double-crossed all the time, though it would seem, if we accept the Porlock-Mycroft identification, that he sometimes suspected it.[1] Sherlock, on the other hand, probably knew exactly where he stood, though he gave his brother plenty of rope—it was characteristic of his bold technique. He ran risks, evidently, from Mycroft's disclosures. For one thing, his appearance was exactly known to the

[1] *The Valley of Fear*, II, 462.

members of Moriarty's gang, though not to Moriarty himself,[1] whereas it was unfamiliar to the general public. John Hector McFarlane ' looked from one to the other of us ' at his first entrance into Baker Street [2]; and the King of Bohemia ' looked from one to the other of us, as if uncertain which to address ' [3]; Dr. Grimesby Roylott asks, ' Which of you is Holmes ? ' [4] and Miss Turner is described as ' glancing from one to the other of us, and finally, *with a woman's quick intuition*, fastening upon my companion.' [5] But Moriarty's emissaries know exactly whom to assault, whom to run down, whose hat to drop bricks on ; they have been carefully primed, evidently by someone who knew him well, with the description of his figure and gait. It will have been Mycroft, too, who supplies Moriarty with the details of Holmes' itinerary in Switzerland,[6] though perhaps—so strange a thing is human nature—consoling himself with the reflection that he was only luring on the arch-criminal to his doom.

It is pleasant to have to record the sequel.

1 *The Final Problem*, I, 541.
2 *The Norwood Builder*, I, 585.
3 *A Scandal in Bohemia*, I, 9.
4 *The Speckled Band*, I, 185.
5 *The Boscombe Valley Mystery*, I, 85 (italics mine).
6 *The Final Problem*, I, 551, 553.

When Colonel Moran had been put away, Mycroft would seem to have dissociated himself altogether from his earlier career of crime, and found the means of making an honest living. It was now, not earlier, that he achieved that curious niche in the Civil Service, which allowed him to co-ordinate the activities of a great Empire, as he had formerly co-ordinated those of a thieves' kitchen. How he achieved it may be plausibly conjectured from what we know of his brother's activities. *The Adventure of the Second Stain* is dated by Mr. Bell in the autumn of 1894, a few months after the Return, a year before *The Bruce-Partington Plans*. The European importance of the services which Sherlock rendered to the Government in the matter of the Trelawny Hope document would make it easy for him to claim a reward from the highest in the land; it was typical of his unselfishness, if all the reward he claimed was a post for his brother, worth £450 a year, enough to provide for his modest needs and keep him out of mischief.

So Mycroft passes from the stage. He is not mentioned in *His Last Bow*, where the appearance on the scene of prominent Government officials would have encouraged us to expect his inter-mediacy. I take it, then, that he did not live to see the Great War, which might, to a man with a

conscience so curiously orientated, have been a
severe test of patriotism. Well for England,
perhaps, that the Intelligence Department of her
chief enemy had to depend on the bungling
methods of a Von Bork. Mycroft died, leaving an
honourable record of faithful service, and his
name is perhaps still breathed with reverence by
the older members of the Diogenes Club. His
secret, buried in the reticent bosom of Sherlock,
can only be pieced together in fragments where,
now and again, Watson has unwittingly stumbled
on the truth. To have probed it will hardly be
counted an indiscretion, in days when so many
biographies are being re-written, and with such
surprising results. He stands before us, as
Watson has painted him for all time : ' His body
was absolutely corpulent, but his face, though
massive, had preserved something of the sharp-
ness of expression which was so remarkable in
that of his brother. His eyes . . . were of a
peculiarly light grey,' and the hand which he
stretched out in welcome was ' a broad, flat hand,
like the flipper of a seal.' [1] A character, you
would be disposed to conjecture, with no great
possibilities for good or evil ; but we have been
taught by a master-mind to distrust such argu-
ments. ' You remember that terrible murderer,

[1] *The Greek Interpreter*, I, 480 f.

Ronald A. Knox

Bert Stevens, who wanted us to get him off in
'87? Was there ever a more mild-mannered,
Sunday-school young man? "[1].   The watery eye,
the flipper-like hand, might deceive the very
elect, but not Sherlock.

[1] *The Norwood Builder*, I, 599.

Mr. Moriarty

A. G. MACDONELL

Dear me, Mr. Holmes ! Dear me.

THE VALLEY OF FEAR

MR. MORIARTY

By far the most important date in the whole saga of 221B Baker Street is the year in which the stranger was killed in Birlstone Manor, Sussex. It is the case which Dr. Watson with his unerring imagery of phrase called *The Valley of Fear*.[1] The reason why the date is of such vital importance is this. If it can be proved that the affair took place at the end of the 'nineties, a whole new glare of light will be thrown upon the character, the moral sense, the intellectual integrity, and the devotion to truth, of Mr. Holmes, and the dog-like loyalty of Dr. Watson to his friend will be emphasised more strongly than ever. There is a definite school of thought which places the date of *The Valley of Fear* in the late 'eighties. If this can be proved, my thesis falls to the ground.

Let us consider the facts.

The earliest date in the story is definite, positive and exact. It was on February 4th, 1875, that Birdy Edwards travelled through the gorges of the Gilmerton Mountains from Stagville to

---

[1] II, 459.

Vermissa.[1] At that date Mr. Edwards was ' not
far from his thirtieth year.' [2] He spent three
months in the Valley, and at the end of that time
he arrested the famous gang of Scowrers. The
date of the trial of the Scowrers may reasonably
be assigned to the autumn of 1875. It could not
have been earlier, for we know that desperate
attempts were made by the accused men to
escape. ' In vain they struggled, in vain the
money of the Lodge was spent like water in the
attempt to save them.' [3] Considering what can
be done with the help of money to delay the
processes of the Law in America, we might be
justified in assuming that the trial lasted on until
1876 or even 1877. But let us be generous. Let
us assume that it was in the autumn of '75 that
McGinty went to the scaffold and Ted Baldwin
to the penitentiary for ten years. On this generous
reckoning Baldwin was released in the autumn of
1885, and it must have been, therefore, in 1886
that Birdy Edwards fled from Chicago and went
to California.

Edwards remained in California more than
five years.[4] This is corroborated by the following
facts :

(1) His first wife died in California.

[1] II, 547.   [3] II, 637.
[2] II, 548.   [4] II, 503.

(2) He was in partnership in California with Douglas for five years, and his wife had died the year before they met.[1]

It could not have been, therefore, earlier than the end of 1892 that Edwards suddenly packed up and came to England.

The reason for his sudden departure was the appearance in the district of Ted Baldwin and his friends, and this took place 'nearer seven years than six'[2] before the date of the killing at Birlstone Manor. This places the date of the killing not earlier than the summer of 1899.

A collateral piece of evidence is found in the age of Birdy Edwards at the time of the case. We are told perfectly clearly by Dr. Watson that Barker, the friend of Edwards (or Douglas, as he called himself at Birlstone), was 'rather younger than Douglas, forty-five at the most.' This would make Edwards about fifty, which would correspond with the fact that he was not far from his thirtieth year in 1875. In other words, he was twenty-six when he went to Vermissa, and fifty at the date of the shooting. This also corresponds with Dr. Watson's estimate that Douglas 'may have been about fifty.'[3]

---

[1] II, 504.
[2] II, 504 f.
[3] II, 479.

M 2

So much for the case that the tragedy at Birlstone could not possibly have taken place earlier than January, 1899, and might even have been later. The case against it depends upon a single sentence in which Dr. Watson, writing of Inspector MacDonald of Scotland Yard, said, ' Those were the early days at the end of the 'eighties.' [1] There is only one way in which this sentence, if accepted, can be made to fit into the remainder of the facts. The original date is positive, the five years in California is positive, the ' nearer seven years than six ' in Europe is positive. There only remains the sentence which Ted Baldwin received. To bring back the date of *The Valley of Fear* from 1899 to 1889, we must assume that Baldwin was released the moment he was convicted, and such a hypothesis is not only dead against the facts as Dr. Watson has recorded them, but is totally out of harmony with the whole spirit of Birdy Edwards' triumph over the Scowrers. It is the whole essence of his brilliant work in the Vermissa Valley in 1875 that he secured convictions and thumping sentences against more than sixty of the gang,[2] and to admit for a moment that Ted Baldwin was released at once is to ruin the structure of the

[1] II, 467.
[2] II, 637.

whole exploit. If, therefore, we are to accept
Dr. Watson's statement that ' those were the early
days at the end of the 'eighties', the whole
structure of the book falls to pieces. It is
impossible that this sentence can be accepted.
And yet it appears on the face of it to be cate-
gorical enough.

Consider this sentence from another angle.
We are asked to believe that at the end of the
'eighties Inspector MacDonald, although a young
man, was a prominent member of Scotland Yard
whom Holmes had already assisted twice in
difficult cases, and who consulted Holmes in
every difficulty.[1] And yet this is the first occasion
on which Dr. Watson ever mentions his name.
The period at the end of the 'eighties was the
period of Lestrade and Gregson. In the case of
the Red-Headed League in 1890 the detective
whom Holmes called in was Mr. Peter Jones
(perhaps a relation of Athelney Jones who
handled the Sign of Four), and in the case of the
Resident Patient the police inspector was called
Lanner. But of an Inspector Alec MacDonald
there is no trace in Dr. Watson's memoirs until
1914, which was the year in which he recorded
the episode of the Valley of Fear. Surely if
Inspector MacDonald had been such a bright

[1] II, 467.

A. G. Macdonell

youth at the end of the 'eighties, consulting Holmes at every turn, we should have heard of him before. The conclusion is irresistible that Watson, never the most accurate of biographers, meant the end of the 'nineties and not the end of the 'eighties. It is much easier to suppose that the worthy doctor made a slip of the pen, rather than that Ted Baldwin got off scot-free.

If I have proved to the satisfaction of the readers of this book that Ted Baldwin was shot at Birlstone Manor not earlier than the beginning of 1899, we find ourselves suddenly in very deep waters. For the information that Edwards (Douglas) was to be attacked by the survivors of the Scowrers came in a cipher message from Fred Porlock, and Fred Porlock was an agent of Mr. Moriarty. Furthermore, two months after Edwards (Douglas) had been acquitted of the charge of shooting Ted Baldwin, he was drowned in a gale off St. Helena, and Holmes definitely announced that he had been murdered by the gang of which Moriarty was the head.[1]

It was in May, 1891, that Mr. Holmes threw Mr. Moriarty over the Reichenbach Fall. How, then, was the retired professor of mathematics out and about in 1899?

There can be only one answer. Moriarty did

[1] II, 639.

not exist. He was invented by Holmes. Or rather Holmes selected a perfectly ordinary ex-professor and fastened on to the unfortunate man the fearful reputation which has dogged him ever since.

The reason why Holmes created this sinister and mysterious colossus of crime was, I submit, as follows. By the middle of the 'eighties he had become, after a difficult early struggle, a highly successful consulting detective. His reputation indeed had already become international, and he was invited to solve mysteries as far afield as Odessa and Trincomalee, where he looked into the tragedy of the Atkinson brothers. But in 1887 he was very seriously ill. He had been working never less than fifteen hours a day for over two months, and on one occasion had worked for five days at a stretch.[1] He had been unravelling, of course, the affairs of the Netherland-Sumatra Company, and the colossal schemes of Baron Maupertuis, and on April 14th of that year Watson was summoned to his sick-bed in Lyons by telegram. The faithful doctor is anxious to lay stress on the comparative slightness of the indisposition. He says he was relieved to find that there was nothing formidable in the symptoms, but it is obvious that from this time

[1] *The Reigate Squires*, I, 417.

for several years the great detective was but a shadow of his former self. It is true that within a few days of returning to London he solved the pretty little problem of the Reigate Squires, but Dr. Watson gives away his own case when he says, 'The year 1887 furnished us with a long series of cases of greater or less interest,'[1] and yet out of all this long series he can only find three that are worth chronicling, and these three are, first the affair at Reigate; secondly, the rather ridiculous episode of the Noble Bachelor; and, thirdly, the case of the Five Orange Pips, in which Holmes failed completely. Doctor Watson mentions a fourth, the Camberwell poisoning case, as having given Holmes a chance of helping in the solution, but the doctor is extremely careful not to go into the details of the affair of the Paradol Chamber, of the Amateur Mendicant Society, the loss of the British barque, *Sophy Anderson*, or of the singular adventure of the Grice Patersons in the island of Uffa.[2] There is another point worth mentioning here. The case of the Five Orange Pips is the first one in which Mr. Holmes tried his hand at excusing himself. He alleged that everything had been completed except the formality of the arrest, but

[1] *The Five Orange Pips*, I, 103.
[2] I, 103.

that the murderers escaped him by being drowned
at sea. So great was his hypnotic influence over
his associates that this explanation was accepted.
Then came another failure, the case of the
Resident Patient, and again Holmes put forward
the same explanation. It had worked once, so
why not again? The three murderers were
drowned in the *Norah Creina*, which was lost
with all hands upon the Portuguese coast, some
leagues to the north of Oporto.[1] The melancholy
tale goes on. Another failure follows at once,
this time in the case of the Greek Interpreter, and
for a third time Holmes spun a yarn to cover
himself up. Feeling presumably that even the
worthy doctor would not swallow a third ship-
wreck, he altered his little fairy-tale into a story
of a stabbing affray in Budapest. So much for
1887.

In 1888 the only recorded case is Holmes'
smashing defeat at the hands of Irene Adler.
In '89 there were only two cases. In the affair of
the Man with the Twisted Lip Holmes made a
ludicrous series of mistakes, and only a sudden
flash of his old brilliance at the very end saved
him from becoming a laughing stock. Shortly
afterwards he completely failed to track down a
party of people in the rural south of England,

[1] *The Resident Patient*, I, 477.

who must have been, to say the least of it, fairly conspicuous. For they consisted of a cart, some heavy boxes, a beautiful woman, an Englishman with a chinchilla beard growing out of the creases of a double-chin, and the terrible Colonel Lysander Stark, who was conspicuous for his thinness.[1] This singular cavalcade had only a few hours' start of Holmes, but he found no clue whatsoever that would lead to their arrest.

This was bad enough in all conscience, but worse was still to follow. In 1890 at a time when a detective, whose room had been literally ankle-deep in telegrams of congratulation in 1887,[2] should have been at the height of his fame and almost too busy to turn round, we find Dr. Watson writing, ' He still came to see me from time to time when he desired a companion in his investigations, but these occasions grew more and more seldom until I find that in the Year 1890 there were only three cases of which I retain any record.' [3] It is painful to have to make the only possible deduction. Either Mr. Holmes had no cases and no clients, or else he did not wish to have a series of failures put upon the records. In October of that year he had one

[1] *The Engineer's Thumb*, I, 206.
[2] *The Reigate Squires*, I, 417.
[3] *The Final Problem*, I, 537.

flicker of intelligence, possibly due to an overdose of cocaine, and the result was the neat capture of John Clay, the founder of the Red-Headed League and the fourth smartest man in London.

Then came the critical year, 1891, in which suddenly, without a word of warning, on April 24th, Mr. Holmes came back from a prolonged holiday in the south of France (there is no corroboration for the newspaper paragraph to the effect that he had been engaged by the French Government on a matter of supreme importance), walked into Dr. Watson's consulting-room and launched the story of ex-Professor Moriarty. The story on the face of it, as he told it on that spring evening was fishy enough in all conscience, but he was well aware, from years of experience, that the good doctor would swallow pretty nearly anything. The story, in effect, was this : that the long series of failures was due not to Holmes' mental decline since his nervous breakdown, but to the existence of a super-criminal, a brain of the first order sitting ' motionless, like a spider in the centre of its web, but that web has a thousand radiations, and he knows well every quiver of each of them.' [1] The man whom Holmes had selected for the part was a real man, a certain mathematical ex-professor who had a great mathe-

[1] *The Final Problem*, I, 540.

matical genius, and who had undoubtedly committed some grave misdemeanour which had led to his expulsion from his University Chair. Note the ingenuity of the explanation. Mr. Moriarty (for he was, of course, no longer a professor) was admittedly a genius; that would account for the all-pervading efficiency of his mythical gang. And there was a dark spot in his life which would effectively prevent him from bringing a slander action against Mr. Holmes.

Dr. Watson swallowed the story at once. He did not inquire how the detective had woven his net round him in London while he was gallivanting about the south of France. He did not ask how Mr. Moriarty got past the vigilance of Mrs. Hudson at 221B when he paid his famous visit to Mr. Holmes. It did not occur to him that Mr. Holmes' description of Mr. Moriarty—' His face protrudes forward, and is for ever slowly oscillating from side to side in a curiously reptilian fashion '[1]—was obviously a sentence that had been written down and learnt by heart. He simply accepted the whole story even to the extent of abandoning his practice and going at once to Switzerland on the journey that was to give the vital verisimilitude to the fairy story, and to rehabilitate the reputation of the great

[1] *The Final Problem*, I, 541.

detective. At Victoria Station Holmes added a neat touch. He saw a tall man pushing his way furiously through the crowd just as the train had begun to move, and he said, 'Ah, there is Moriarty himself.' The doctor accepted that as he accepted everything else. Another neat touch was the despatch of the special train to follow the Continental express. Probably it contained Mycroft Holmes.

The final scene was brilliantly stage-managed. Once again no one except Sherlock saw Moriarty, and the great detective was free to regain his health by travelling in Tibet, passing through Persia, looking in at Mecca, and amusing himself in researches into coal-tar derivatives in Montpelier,[1] secure in the knowledge that his reputation, so far from being diminished by his series of failures, was enormously enhanced by his success in ridding the world of the master criminal.

Feeling himself fully restored in 1894, he returned to London and resumed his practice.

* * * * *

We have now arrived at a deadlock. How is it explainable that the world thought that Mr. Moriarty was killed in 1891 and yet accepted without question his existence in 1899? There

[1] *The Empty House*, I, 569.

can be only one explanation. Between '94 and '99 it must have occurred to Holmes that the occasion might arise a second time in which he would have need of an excuse for covering up failures, and he decided to resuscitate Moriarty. The unfortunate lecturer, therefore, was dragged out of the retirement into which Holmes must have blackmailed him in '91, in order to account for his disappearance, and settled him down with a comfortable income and a house in the suburbs, to remain there and carry on his work as a mathematical lecturer until such time as Holmes might have need of him again. The explanation of how Moriarty survived the mythical wrestling match above the Reichenbach Fall would be simple. Just as Holmes clung to one rock, so Moriarty might be presumed to have clung to another. And by 1899, when the old crowd at the Yard, who had been deceived by the first bluff, had all retired and been succeeded by men like MacDonald, the opportunity was ripe for working the bluff again. So inefficient were the Yard officers of the period that the story of 1891 had not been handed on in the records to the officers of 1899, for Inspector MacDonald, at this latter date, accepted implicitly Holmes' statement that he had never seen Moriarty.

There is, so far as I can see, no other possible explanation that covers the facts.

The whole story throws a somewhat lurid light upon the character of the great detective. Vanity was his besetting foible, and his creation of the super-criminal was simply due to his passionate desire not to appear a fool in the eyes of the world, and especially of Scotland Yard. That he suffered some twinges of remorse for his treatment of the unfortunate Army Coach is shown by his present to him of the picture by Greuze. For it must have been Holmes, of course, who gave it to him.

But, after all, Vanity is a very human weakness, and much may be forgiven to such a man.

Sherlock Holmes and the Fair Sex

S. C. ROBERTS

*I am glad of all details, whether they seem
to you to be relevant or not.*

THE COPPER BEECHES

SHERLOCK HOLMES AND THE
FAIR SEX

CERTAIN imaginative playwrights, with a greater regard for popular sentiment than for documentary evidence, have boldly portrayed Sherlock Holmes not only as a lover, but as husband and father. To the ordinary playgoer such conjectural creations may afford a pleasant evening's entertainment; but, in the eyes of serious students of the literature of Baker Street, they are a wholly unworthy tribute to the man who cried 'Give me data'; furthermore they tend to obscure the more pressing problems of Bakerian scholarship.

At the same time a careful re-examination of the whole question of Holmes' attitude towards the fair sex may well be regarded as one of the major *desiderata*. Granted the unreality which must characterise any picture of Holmes in the conventional bliss of domesticity, have not scholars in the past been too prone to uncritical acceptance of Holmes as misogynist? For this view Watson himself is, no doubt, principally responsible. Having stated categorically in *The*

N 2

Sign of Four the grounds of Holmes' objections to matrimony (' Love is an emotional thing . . . opposed to that true, cold reason which I place above all things. I should never marry myself, lest I bias my judgment '),[1] he proceeds in *A Scandal in Bohemia* to elaborate his theme :

' It was not that he felt any emotion akin to love for Irene Adler. All emotions, and that one particularly, were abhorrent to his cold, precise, but admirably balanced mind. He was, I take it, the most perfect reasoning and observing machine that the world has seen : but, as a lover, he would have placed himself in a false position. He never spoke of the softer passions, save with a gibe and a sneer. They were admirable things for the observer—excellent for drawing the veil from men's motives and actions. But for the trained reasoner to admit such intrusions into his own delicate and finely adjusted temperament was to introduce a distracting factor which might throw a doubt upon all his mental results. Grit in a sensitive instrument, or a crack in one of his own high-power lenses, would not be more disturbing than a strong emotion in a nature such as his.' [2]

It is noteworthy that this characterisation belongs to a period in which Watson was absorbed in the new-found happiness of his own first marriage, the happiness which lies in the ' home-centred interests which rise up around the man who first finds himself master of his own establishment.' At such a time Holmes

[1] II, 270.
[2] I, 3.

appeared to him as one who ' loathed every form of society with his whole Bohemian soul,' and it was inevitable that Watson, the literary artist, should heighten the contrast. But Watson's artistry must not be allowed to mislead us. We must look upon other pictures of Holmes than these impressionist sketches of Holmes the Confirmed Misogynist and Holmes the Complete Bohemian. Before a true judgment upon Holmes' relations with women can properly be passed, it is necessary to review a larger body of evidence and to review it in such a spirit of scientific detachment as Holmes himself would have approved.

It is, of course, true that Holmes was ' never a very sociable fellow.' Victor Trevor was the only friend he made at college, but he was a ' close friend ' and a real ' bond of union ' was formed between them. The nature of the common ground on which they met is also worth remark : ' He [Trevor] was as friendless as I,' [1] Holmes rather wistfully records. May not Holmes have belonged to that class of persons—a class larger than is commonly realised—who fervently and secretly rejoice in congenial society, but are debarred by deep-seated inhibitions from making the initiatory step in a social rapprochement ?

[1] *The ' Gloria Scott,'* I, 375.

To the peculiar significance of Holmes' further
relations with Trevor we shall return later. For
the moment it may be worth while to recall
Holmes' eagerness to secure a fellow-lodger in
No. 221B Baker Street. It is true that the recorded
motive is a financial one, but no one funda-
mentally unsociable would have taken the risk,
especially with a complete stranger, of setting up
a joint establishment. Clearly, Holmes was glad
of company, even before the development of his
personal affection for Watson himself. In the
early days, to put the case at its lowest, Watson's
company was a solace when clients were few and
far between. Holmes abominated the ' dull
routine of existence '; he craved for ' mental
exaltation ' and this exaltation could only come
from the study of his fellow human beings. For
it would be a mistake to regard Holmes as being
devoted to scientific investigation for its own
sake. To him the laboratory was a means, not an
end. His famous discovery of a reagent precipitated exclusively by hæmoglobin thrilled him not
as an addition to chemical knowledge, but as ' the
most practical medico-legal discovery for years.' [1]
When he had no case in hand, Holmes, so far
from filling his leisure happily with independent
laboratory research, was obliged, much to Wat-

[1] *A Study in Scarlet*, II, 10.

son's distress, to have recourse to artificial stimulants. While he might, in the Johnsonian sense, have been described as an 'unclubable' man, he was, nevertheless, as incapable of supporting a mental solitude as Johnson himself. Like Johnson, he was, in his own way, obliged to anyone who visited him. If no clients rang the bell of No. 221B Baker Street, Holmes would console himself with his Boswell, whom he admitted to be indispensable.

So much, then, may be said by way of introduction and by way of dispelling the notion that Holmes was by nature a recluse. Of his attitude towards women in particular we have, fortunately, a very considerable body of evidence.

Among the early adventures none stands out more clearly than *The Speckled Band*. At the outset Holmes greets Miss Stoner with a cheerfulness which betokens his satisfaction at the initiation of a new problem. Watson is introduced and hot coffee is ordered for the lady. But it was no time for the ' exchange of social pleasantries.'

' It is not cold which makes me shiver,' said the woman in a low voice, changing her seat as requested.

' What then ? '

' It is fear, Mr. Holmes. It is terror.' [1]

---

[1] I, 174.

At once Holmes' manner changes :

' You must not fear,' [1] he says, soothingly, and, bending forward he pats the poor girl's forearm. Little wonder that Miss Stoner's heart was lightened when she left Baker Street. Holmes' sympathy had been of no merely formal kind— he had pressed her to stay to breakfast. The affair of the Speckled Band was, as Watson quickly deduced, ' a most dark and sinister business.' [2] At Stoke Moran Holmes' protective- ness in regard to Miss Stoner is again evident. Naturally the poor girl was overjoyed to see her friends. Quickly she began to follow the working of Holmes' mind : ' I believe, Mr. Holmes, that you have already made up your mind.' [3] Further, she was not afraid to lay her hand upon the detective's sleeve. ' Good-bye and be brave,' was Holmes' parting injunction as, with Watson by his side, he left Miss Stoner on the fateful night when Dr. Grimesby Roylott's villainies met with their most fitting punishment ; finally, Holmes accompanied Watson in breaking the news to the terrified girl and in conveying her to the care of her good aunt of Harrow.

In *A Case of Identity*, again, Miss Mary Suther-

[1] I, 175.
[2] I, 184.
[3] I, 193.

land's troubles aroused, in the first instance, little more than a professional interest in Holmes' mind. 'Oscillation upon the pavement,' he told the wondering Watson, 'always means an *affaire du cœur*. . . . When a woman has been seriously wronged by a man she no longer oscillates, and the usual symptom is a broken bell wire.' [1]

Miss Sutherland enters the room. Holmes greets her with the 'easy courtesy' of the professional consultant. But as her story is unfolded, he displays a warmth of feeling far beyond the limits of dispassionate inquiry. 'You have been very shamefully treated,' [2] he cries at one point, and the advice he gives her at the conclusion of the interview has reference to the girl's own peace of mind rather than to the problem of the missing bridegroom. As he frankly confessed to Watson, he found the girl more interesting than the case. The case, indeed, held little of novelty or attraction for Holmes; he had come across similar affairs at Andover and at The Hague. It was Mary Sutherland who engrossed his attention, and, later, it was no mere passion for justice in the abstract, but the throbbing pulse of human sympathy that made him long to lay a horsewhip across the shoulders of the scoundrelly James

[1] I, 58.
[2] I, 63.

Windibank. Holmes' final comment on the case reveals a profundity of insight into feminine psychology :

'If I tell her she will not believe me. You may remember the old Persian saying, " There is danger for him who taketh the tiger cub, and danger also for whoso snatches a delusion from a woman." ' [1]

It was a maxim that was later to receive a terrible confirmation in the case of *The Illustrious Client*.

Evidences of the affectionate feelings which Holmes entertained from time to time towards his lady clients peep out from Watson's narrative. It is to Watson, of course, that we normally owe the more detailed descriptions of feminine dress and appearance. Mrs. St. Clair, for instance, was ' a little blonde woman . . . clad in some sort of light *mousseline-de-soie*, with a touch of fluffy pink chiffon at her neck and wrists. She stood,' Watson continues, ' with her figure outlined against the flood of light, one hand upon the door, one half raised in eagerness, her body slightly bent, her head and face protruded, with eager eyes and parted lips, a standing question.' [2]

[1] I, 75.
[2] I, 137 f.

A careless reading of *The Man with the Twisted Lip* might suggest that such a vision had no effect upon the apostle of ' true, cold reason.' But it was Holmes who confessed : ' I was wondering what I should say to this dear little woman to-night ' ; it was Holmes who told Neville St. Clair that he would have done better to have trusted his wife.

Instinctively Holmes was quick to grasp the woman's point of view, as the unfortunate Lord Robert St. Simon [1] discovered. Holmes, indeed, could ' hardly see how the lady could have acted otherwise ' than vanish at the wedding breakfast. She was, as he said, motherless and had no one to advise her in a crisis.

' It was a slight, sir, a public slight,' protested the noble bachelor.

' You must make allowance for this poor girl,' was Holmes' reply, and the supper ordered from outside to do honour to the lady was of a quality unprecedented in the annals of 221B Baker Street.[2]

Once, when Holmes received a request for

[1] Holmes' repeated reference to 'Lord St. Simon' is a curious solecism; it may perhaps be due to carelessness on Watson's part when he put his notes into narrative form.

[2] A couple of brace of cold woodcock, a pheasant, a *pâté-de-foie-gras* pie, with a group of ancient and cobwebby bottles.' (I, 240.)

187

advice about the offer of a post as governess, he petulantly complained of the triviality of the application :

'As to my own little practice,' he broke out to Watson, 'it seems to be degenerating into an agency for recovering lost lead pencils and giving advice to young ladies from boarding-schools. I think that I have touched bottom at last . . .' [1]

But when Miss Violet Hunter ('with a bright quick face freckled like a plover's egg' as Watson vividly describes her) appeared at Baker Street in person, it was at once apparent that Holmes was favourably impressed. Later, when Miss Hunter's story of her experience at the Copper Beeches had been told, Holmes was moved to warm and un-stinted praise : 'You seem to me,' he declared, 'to have acted all through this matter like a brave and sensible girl.' [2] So marked, indeed, was Holmes' admiration that Watson expresses his disappointment that Holmes should have mani-fested no further interest in the girl after they had safely conducted her to Winchester. Why should Watson be disappointed ? It cannot, surely, have been on his own account.[3] He was a married

---

[1] *The Copper Beeches*, I, 277.
[2] I, 297.
[3] In this connection I cannot accept Mr. H. W. Bell's inferences (*Sherlock Holmes and Dr. Watson*, p. 68).

man at the time, and, though his wife's health was probably failing, it is not to be imagined that he had taken anything more than a comradely interest in Violet Hunter. Why, then, if we are to accept Watson's own picture of his friend as 'loathing every form of society with his whole Bohemian soul,' should he be surprised at Holmes losing interest in the lady as soon as her problem had been solved? We are driven to conclude that Watson had been so strongly impressed by Holmes' unusually warm regard for Miss Hunter that he hoped that the friendship might ripen and develop.[1]

Harshness, as Watson says, was foreign to Holmes' nature, and when a 'young and beautiful woman, tall, graceful, and queenly'[2] broke in upon the investigation of the abstruse and complicated problem of John Vincent Harden, the tobacco magnate, Holmes, a little put out at first, begged the beautiful intruder to take a seat. As the lady's story was unfolded, he quickly grew sympathetic.

'Oh, Cyril is his name!'[3] he broke in archly at one point; and when Violet Smith had gone,

---

[1] Miss Hunter became head of a school at Walsall. It is possible that the whole Birmingham area held a measure of poignancy for Holmes (see below, p. 194.)

[2] *The Solitary Cyclist*, I, 640.

[3] I, 641.

he had no doubt about her charm : ' It is part of the settled order of Nature that such a girl should have followers,' [1] he said, pulling at a meditative pipe.   For a time he was uncertain whether Miss Smith's troubles would prove to be anything more than a trivial affair, but after a fuller investigation he quickly changed his view : ' It is our duty,' he told Watson, ' to see that no one molests her upon that last journey.' [2]   Just as Holmes was constantly moved to compassionate as well as professional interest by the distress of a defenceless girl, so he showed an extreme warmth, as well as a nice delicacy, of feeling in regard to any disaster which might threaten to wreck a happy marriage.   The dialogue between him and the unfortunate Lady Hilda Trelawney Hope is one of the most dramatic in the whole series of adventures.·

' She stood grandly defiant,' writes Watson, ' a queenly figure, her eyes fixed upon his as if she would read his very soul.'   But the defiance could not last and before long she was at Holmes' feet, ' her beautiful face upturned and wet with her tears.'   Gently raising her, he uttered no word of reproach, but quietly expressed his thankfulness for her eleventh-hour confession.

[1] I, 645.
[2] I, 651.

All her defences down, the lady told her whole story: 'Put yourself in my position, Mr. Holmes! What was I to do?' The reply was the same as the advice given to Neville St. Clair: 'Take your husband into your confidence . . .' Holmes' satisfaction in protecting Lady Hilda's secret was evident. 'We also have our diplomatic secrets,' he told the Prime Minister.[1]

But nowhere in the depth of Holmes' feeling for the sanctity of feminine beauty and innocence more eloquently revealed than in the famous story of *The Illustrious Client*:

'I don't quite know how to make her [Violet de Merville] clear to you, Watson. Perhaps you may meet her before we are through, and you can use your own gift of words. She is beautiful, but with the ethereal other-world beauty of some fanatic whose thoughts are set on high. I have seen such faces in the pictures of the old masters of the Middle Ages.'[2]

In vain he pleaded with her as he would have pleaded with a daughter of his own. The occasion spurred him to unwonted eloquence. Emotion triumphed over intellect, and every degree of warmth of which he was capable was concentrated in his appeal:

'I pictured to her,' as he told Watson, 'the awful position of the woman who only wakes to a man's

[1] *The Second Stain*, I, 881–7.
[2] I, 1102.

191

character after she is his wife—a woman who has to submit to be caressed by bloody hands and lecherous lips. . . . " [1]

Seldom indeed was Holmes keyed to so melodramatic a pitch ; and it was only the spectacle of a wronged and beautiful woman that could so move him.[2]

The same feeling is manifested in the well-known story of *Charles Augustus Milverton*, and there are few more tender passages in the literature of Baker Street than that at the conclusion of *The Veiled Lodger*, when Holmes was impelled to make one of his rare comments on the riddle of the universe : ' Poor girl ! ' he cried. ' The ways of Fate are indeed hard to understand. If there is not some compensation hereafter, then the world is a cruel jest.' [3] With his quick intuition,

[1] I, 1103.

[2] Elsewhere (*Dr. Watson*, p. 27 f) I have suggested that Miss de Merville afterwards became the second wife of Dr. Watson. Critics have dismissed this theory as fantastic or even as negligible, sometimes with a greater measure of scorn than of argument. The objection that Watson would not have cared to record his wife's early misfortunes is certainly valid, but it should be remembered (*a*) that the story was not published for twenty years after the events described ; (*b*) that Watson may have disguised the surnames in his narrative. If my theory is correct, it may well be that the unusually fervid description owes something to Watson's own feelings.

[3] I, 1299.

he observed something significant in the voice of
Eugenia Ronder as she came to the end of her
tragic story :

> 'Your life is not your own,' he said. 'Keep your
> hands off it.'
> 'What use is it to anyone ?'
> 'How can you tell ? The example of patient suffering
> is in itself the most precious of all lessons to an impatient
> world.'[1]

As is well known, Holmes' solemn injunction
had its effect. The brave woman ('the poor
wounded beast that had crawled into its hole to
die') took the detective's counsel and with it
fresh courage.

Such examples as these—and doubtless they
could be supplemented—of Holmes' tenderness
and sensibility in his relations with women are
surely of some significance. At the very least
their cumulative effect is to dispel the common
impression that Holmes was a misogynist or that
women only interested him as 'cases.' Of course,
like any specialist, Holmes approached his clients
in the first instance from a purely professional
angle, but again and again we have evidence that
this professional interest was supplemented and
intensified by a quick and intuitive sympathy
evoked, more often than not, by the tale of a

---

[1] I, 1299 f.

woman's distress. When his heart was thus
touched, he did not, except in rare cases, elaborate
the theme in conversation with Watson. Watson,
indeed, was no doubt misled, as many of his
readers have been misled, by the measure of
Holmes' more expansive comment on Irene
Adler. 'To Sherlock Holmes she was always
the woman.' But this is a purely intellectual
tribute—an outburst of admiration for the
woman who outwitted him. To the scale of
Holmes' emotional values it has no kind of
relevance.

If, then, we are right in crediting Holmes with
a more lively understanding of the feminine point
of view than has been heretofore assumed, are
there elements in the background of his life which
would tend to substantiate this fresh conception
of the great detective's emotional make-up? It
must be admitted at once that the material is
slight. Of Holmes' relations the only one
definitely known to us is Mycroft; his ancestors
were country squires of orthodox habits; one
of his grandmothers (presumably on his mother's
side) was French and the sister of an artist. As
an undergraduate, as we have seen, he had only
one intimate friend—Victor Trevor. Now when
Trevor invited Holmes to his father's country
house in Norfolk, Holmes appears to have

accepted the invitation with alacrity, and he stayed not a week-end, but a month. There was good fishing and duck-shooting, a good library and good food, and Holmes makes no disguise of the fact that life was pleasant at Donnithorpe. He proceeds to explain that Victor Trevor was an only son, that his father was a widower and that his sister was dead : ' There had been a daughter, I heard, but she had died of diphtheria while on a visit to Birmingham.' [1] This is a curious sentence. The fact of Trevor senior (*alias* James Armitage) having had a daughter as well as a son has little or no relevance to the story of the *Gloria Scott*. That Holmes should mention the daughter in describing the Donni-thorpe household to Watson is, perhaps, natural enough. But why should he particularise both the nature and the occasion of her death ? ' She had died of diphtheria while on a visit to Birming-ham.' Why—one is bound to press the question —did Holmes suddenly recall the circumstantial and, on the face of it, second-hand details about the decease of his friend's sister ? But were they, in fact, second-hand ? Is it possible that Holmes' pluperfect is just an emotional camouflage ? It will be remembered that after his father's death Victor Trevor went out to be a tea-planter in the

[1] I, 376.

Terai and that Holmes kept in touch with him. Assuming, for the moment, that Trevor's sister was in fact alive at the time of her father's tragic death, she would naturally spend some time after the melancholy event among friends or relations. Assuming, further, that Holmes' specific, and yet wholly superfluous reference, conceals an indication of some closer interest than is conveyed in the bald sentence in the narrative of *The 'Gloria Scott'*,[1] are we not justified in the conjecture, to put it no higher, that Holmes was in fact attracted to Miss Trevor and that his hopes and affections were rudely shattered by the ravages of diphtheria in Birmingham in the 'seventies ?[2]

It is not difficult to imagine how, after such an annihilation of his early hopes, Holmes would for the time renounce the whole race of women except in so far as they might be of promise, or of

[1] Mr. H. W. Bell (*Sherlock Holmes and Dr. Watson*, pp. 7 ff) points out a number of inconsistencies in the story of James Armitage and concludes either that Holmes was too young and impressionable to subject it to critical analysis or that ' in a freakish mood ' he concocted the story himself. It would appear more likely that Holmes deliberately varied certain parts of the whole narrative in order to conceal its importance in his own emotional history.

[2] The average death-rate per 1,000 of the population from diphtheria in the 'seventies was ·43 as compared with ·03 in 1932. (Information kindly supplied by the Medical Officer of Health of Birmingham.)

service, in the profession of scientific detection. His was just such a nature as would, after a severe disappointment in youth, react violently from the cultivation of female society. Here may be found the true explanation of the elevation of the ' true, cold reason ' which Holmes placed above all things. It is the typical reaction, familiar to all psychologists, of frustrated desire. Further, it seems extremely probable that one of the more tragic symptoms of this reaction is to be found in the cocaine habit, which was an object of very natural distress to Watson. Here it is worth while recalling some passages in the well-known dialogue at the end of *The Sign of Four*. When Watson announced his engagement, Holmes gave a most dismal groan and refused to congratulate his friend. Naturally Watson was a little hurt. Had Holmes anything against the lady ?

' Not at all,' was the reply. ' I think she is one of the most charming young ladies I ever met . . . ' [1] Watson was relieved, but noted that Holmes looked weary. Yes, Holmes admitted, the reaction was already upon him ; there came over him, too, the wistful dualism of Goethe. Why had Nature made but *one* man out of the stuff whereof he himself was fashioned ?

[1] II, 270.

He could, he reflected, have been a ' pretty spry
sort of fellow.' [1] Finally the good-hearted
Watson declared :

' The division seems rather unfair. You have
done all the work in this business. I get a wife
out of it, Jones gets the credit ; pray what
remains for you ? '

' For me,' said Sherlock Holmes, ' there
remains the cocaine-bottle.' [2] If we are justified
in our conjecture concerning Holmes' previous
history,[3] does not this whole passage assume a
new sadness and a new significance ?

' Work,' as Holmes himself remarked to
Watson on a later occasion, ' is the best antidote
to sorrow ' [4]; and with the passing of years it is
noteworthy that we read less about cocaine and
more about the geniality, and even tenderness, of
Holmes' relations with the fair sex.[5]

[1] II, 271.
[2] Loc. cit.
[3] Holmes was a good actor, and it would be unfair to
adduce his engagement to Milverton's housemaid as
important evidence ; but it may be remarked that he
appears to have played his part with a total lack of
embarrassment.
[4] *The Empty House*, I, 569.
[5] It would be interesting to discover the Christian name
of Victor Trevor's sister. I conjecture that it was Violet.
It is noteworthy that this name belonged to three ladies
(Miss Hunter, Miss Smith and Miss de Merville) whom
Holmes treated with more than ordinary courtesy.

In the quest of the whole truth of the inner history of Sherlock Holmes the thesis presented here cannot claim to be more than an essay in exploration; but one thing is certain: Holmes cannot, on a proper examination of the evidence, be any longer regarded as the embodiment of asexual ratiocination.

The Date of 'The Sign of Four'

H. W. BELL

> 'The date?' asked Holmes, opening his note-book.
>
> THE SIGN OF FOUR

THE DATE OF *THE SIGN OF FOUR*

THE date of *The Sign of Four* is of primary importance in the chronology of Sherlock Holmes' activities. All students of the subject recognise the urgency of settling it once and for all ; and yet with the passage of time the problem has become confused rather than clarified. This paper is an attempt to show that the true date of the occurrences related is from September 27th to 30th 1887.[1]

(I) THE MONTH.—In Chapter II [2] Watson quotes Holmes, who has been examining the letter received by Miss Morstan, as saying : 'Post-mark, London, S.W. Date, July 7.' In Chapter III,[3] however, which continues the incidents of the same day, Watson records that 'it was a September evening.'

Here at the outset is a contradiction. Though there is no further mention of the month by name, we are told that 'a dense drizzly fog lay

[1] Rather than September 7th–8th, as we proposed in *Sherlock Holmes and Dr. Watson*, p. 38.

[2] II, 155.

[3] II, 160.

low upon the great city,'[1] and that it was 'a yellow fog.'[2] At the end of Chapter IX, Holmes, before setting out to capture Jonathan Small, provides a dinner of 'oysters and a brace of grouse.'[3] The weight of evidence is heavily in favour of September, since neither fog nor menu belong in July.

At this point we must pause to examine an objection which has recently been made.[4] ' " It had just struck three on the Palace Clock " when Watson came back to Pondicherry Lodge with the invaluable Toby. Holmes climbs out on to the roof and down a water pipe, and the chase starts ; " the east had been gradually whitening, and we could now see some distance in the cold grey light." . . . Was this meant to be Sept. 8,[5] when the sun rises at 5.24, or on July 8, when the sun rises at 3.53 ? ' It is true that on September 8th the sun rises at 5.24 (on the 28th the time is 5.56) ; but the important moment is not sunrise but daybreak, which on the 28th occurs at about

[1] Loc. cit.
[2] II, 151.
[3] II, 226.
[4] R. A. Knox, in *New Statesman* (November 12th, 1932).
[5] Father Knox's objection to our retaining (see *Sherlock Holmes and Dr. Watson*, p. 50) the day of the month (the 7th) as reported by Watson for the beginning of the adventure while rejecting the month itself (July) is logical, and is strengthened by evidence to be considered later.

4.2.[1] Furthermore, it should be observed that Father Knox allows far too brief a time for Holmes' activities at Pondicherry Lodge between Watson's return with Toby and the start of the chase.[2] First, the dog was tied to the hall table; then Holmes and Watson mounted to the top floor, where Holmes took off his shoes and stockings. This done, they clambered up into the garret where they spent some time examining and discussing the footprints in the dust. Watson was then sent hurrying downstairs and out of doors, where he looked up and saw Holmes moving along the roof ' like an enormous glow-worm.' Holmes was ' crawling very slowly,' and when at last he slid down to the ground and put on his stockings and shoes again a considerable time had elapsed since Watson's arrival with Toby at 3 a.m. It could not have been before 3.45 that they started forth with Toby, about a quarter of an hour before daybreak.

This suits the narrative. Consider the conditions in July. On the 8th, when the sun rises at 3.54, it has has been light for a long time (in fact, there is no closed night in July in the latitude of

[1] On October 1st daybreak is at 4.8. The change during September is at the rate of about two minutes each day.
[2] II, 196–8.

London until after the 21st), and the bull's-eye lantern which Watson remembered so vividly, making Holmes look like an enormous glow-worm as he moved slowly along the roof, would not have been especially noticeable to a person standing on the ground. And, finally, it should be observed that the appearance of the sun, some time after their start, is actually mentioned.[1] Their rate of progress was slow : Holmes himself speaks of it as ' a six-mile limp for a half-pay officer with a damaged tendo Achillis.' [2]

The other objection which Father Knox raises is based upon the statement, on the last day of the adventure, that ' as we passed the City the last rays of the sun were gilding the cross upon the summit of St. Paul's,' [3] in the neighbourhood of 7.30. On July 10th the sun does not set until 8.13, and on September 30th the time is 5.40. Here again is a difficulty which is perhaps not insoluble. Athelney Jones had arrived in Baker Street at three o'clock. After he had had a short conversation with Watson, Holmes turned up in disguise, at about 3.15. There was some further talk, as a result of which Jones had to ' step across

[1] ' Now the red rim of the sun pushes itself over the London cloud-bank.' This, of course, was later than the actual time of sunrise.

[2] See *Note on Dr. Watson's Wound*, below, p. 218.

[3] II, 231.

the road and telephone,' but not until Holmes had made him promise to return for dinner in ' half an hour.' On that day, therefore, the dinner-hour cannot have been later than four o'clock. The meal, as we know, was a short one, and in spite of the variety of subjects upon which Holmes discoursed—probably very rapidly, for ' he appeared to be in a state of nervous exaltation '—it could easily have been over by 4.45.[1] Thus they could have arrived at Westminster Wharf at a little after five, and not after seven,[2] as the text has it, and in consequence the sunset would fit perfectly a date at the end of September. The extant text fits neither July nor September. The net result, then, of these two objections is that the first is found to point unmistakably to the autumn, and that the second, which is impossible as it stands, may plausibly be altered to fit that season, since it cannot be reconciled with a date in the month of July.[3]

(II) THE DAY.—Father Knox objects to our

---

[1] II, 222–7.

[2] It is quite possible for a crabbed hand to write ' five ' so that it resembles ' seven.' Miss Dorothy L. Sayers has suggested (' The Dates in *The Red-Headed League*,' *Colophon*, vol. v, pt. 17, 1934) that Watson did not dot his ' i's.'

[3] It is most unlikely that Jones would have remained in Baker Street from 3 p.m. until dinner if that meal had not been served before 5.30 or 6.

estimate of the 'time occupied' (from Wednesday, September 7th to Thursday, the 8th). We admit the miscalculation; but in his own counter-suggestion he is himself at fault.

The order of events is as follows (the days are designated by letters in order not to prejudge the results):

(A) Bartholomew Sholto discovers the treasure and notifies Thaddeus, who goes to Norwood and tells his brother that he intends to communicate with Miss Morstan. The confederate in Bartholomew's house informs Jonathan Small.

(B) At about 3 a.m. Small visits Mordecai Smith, and they go away in the launch. Miss Morstan receives Thaddeus' letter, and calls upon Holmes after luncheon. At 6 p.m. she returns and goes with Holmes and Watson *via* the Lyceum Theatre to Thaddeus' house. Later, they all drive to Norwood, where they find Bartholomew murdered and the treasure gone.

(C) Episode of the dog Toby, and discovery of Smith's wharf. Mrs. Smith says that her husband has been absent since 'yesterday mornin'.

(D) Watson records little of this day.

(E) End of the chase.

From Holmes' advertisement it is clear that Mordecai Smith departed with his launch 'at or about three o'clock last Tuesday morning.'

Therefore (B) = Tuesday, and not Monday, as Father Knox suggests; and the capture was effected on Friday.[1]

The day on which the adventure began can be determined with a high degree of probability from a study of Watson's handwriting. Elsewhere, Miss Dorothy L. Sayers has demonstrated, in a brilliant piece of reconstructive criticism which rivals Theobald's famous discovery of ' A babbled of greene fields,' under the farrago ' A table of greene fields,' how when the doctor's crabbed handwriting was transcribed, ' August 4 ' was taken to be ' April 27.'[2] We suggest that when his account of *The Sign of Four* was being written out from his notes a hieroglyphic like

$$Ju7$$

intended for ' S27 ' was taken to be ' Ju7.'

(III) THE YEAR.—Mr. T. S. Blakeney, in defending his gallant raid upon the traditional chronology of *The Sign of Four*, contends that he has found in it indications which point with

[1] Father Knox (loc. cit.) shows conclusively that the capture could not have taken place on Saturday.

[2] Op. cit.

certainty to 1888.[1] Chief among these are the
various references to ' six years ago ' which occur
in the story, the references all being to 1882.
Since the dating which he advocates, 1888,
clashes with the number of Miss Morstan's pearls,[2]
he suggests that she had really received seven, and
that the first had been ' made up into a brooch or
pendant.'   Father Knox, when attempting to
strengthen the 1888 theory, dismisses this explanation, but proposes in its place an even more
curious one ; he maintains that Miss Morstan
did not know when she had actually received her
first pearl ! To quote an author much in favour
with the distinguished cleric : ' On such matters
one does not deceive oneself ' ; and in view of
Holmes' expressed opinion of her intelligence
and of her potential ' value in our work,' the
suggestion was not, perhaps, advanced seriously.
His further notion that the Sholto brothers would
have had to prove their father's Will before
sending the first pearl, thereby necessarily delay-
ing the despatching of it by a year, reveals a
profound misconception of their attitude. They
were a lawless lot. Major Sholto had come dis-

---

[1] *Sherlock Holmes : Fact or Fiction ?* pp. 54 ff.
[2] She told Holmes that she had received one every May,
beginning with 1882. She had six at the time the adventure
begins.

honestly by the treasure ; he had quarrelled with his crony over the division of it, and is not unsuspected of having killed him ; his son Bartholomew wished to keep it entirely for himself and his brother ; and even Sholto, who alone of the family had some generous impulses, was insistent that ' no outsiders—no police or officials' should be brought into the affair, adding significantly : ' We can settle everything satisfactorily among ourselves, without any interference.' [1] He had no intention of becoming involved with the Treasury. The chaplet had undoubtedly been concealed by the brothers after their father's death, and the delay which Father Knox postulates before the pearl could have been sent exists solely in his own imagination.

But the difficulty of the ' six years ' remains. We suggest that the explanation is to be found once more in Watson's handwriting, and that he made his 5 thus, 5, without the horizontal bar, a form of the numeral which, as we know from experience, is sometimes seen. It is easily mistaken for 6, and was doubtless so interpreted by the compositor.

In addition to the internal data which we have been considering, there are the external data.

Mr. Blakeney is drastic in his treatment of *A*

[1] II, 165.

Scandal in Bohemia. But it is straining the probabilities beyond the breaking-point to maintain that in this, the first in Watson's earliest collection of short stories, he should have blundered over the year. The date as transmitted to us does indeed contain an error, which we would reconcile with the other facts by a correction of two days. Mr. Blakeney is obliged, on his theory, to alter it by three hundred and sixty-five, and even then cannot make it fit the evidence.[1]

He further insists that the 1887 dating ' clashes with every other date in the record. The traditional dates for *The Noble Bachelor* and *A Scandal in Bohemia*, it is true, fit in with 1887, but *The Five Orange Pips* would need to be put forward one year at least ; neither *The Engineer's Thumb* nor *The Man with the Twisted Lip* will fit, and great difficulties arise with *The Resident Patient, The Cardboard Box* and *The Crooked Man.* The required correlation of *A Scandal in Bohemia, A Case of Identity, The Man with the Twisted Lip* and *The Blue Carbuncle* is set at naught.'[2]

[1] He is at once involved in difficulties, and therefore proposes (op. cit., p. 59) to ' exclude the Sunday from the " working " days.' On what grounds ? Was Holmes a Sabbatarian ? And why quotation-marks around ' working ' ? The word is not in the text, as, from the inverted commas, the unwary might imagine.

[2] Op. cit., pp. 62 f.

It is quite true that the dates given in *The Five Orange Pips* do not fit the traditional date of the marriage. On our own schedule it need not be advanced more than one year, i.e., from 1887 to 1888 ; but in order to accord with Mr. Blakeney's hypothesis it must be moved two years, to 1889. There is no difficulty about *The Man with the Twisted Lip*, with Watson's dating of which (1889) no one has yet taken issue. Neither is there any trouble about *The Crooked Man*. *The Cardboard Box* is not relevant. Watson quotes Holmes as referring in it to *A Study in Scarlet* and *The Sign of Four*, ' which you have chronicled.' [1] Since the latter was first published in February, 1890, some years after Watson's marriage, it is probable that the affair of *The Cardboard Box* occurred in August, 1890,[2] at a time when Watson was temporarily occupying his old room in Baker Street.

The ' required correlation of *A Scandal in Bohemia*, *A Case of Identity*, *The Man with the Twisted Lip* and *The Blue Carbuncle*,' [3] which Mr. Blakeney believes so important, is set at naught by his own schedule. In the last-mentioned story

[1] I, 936.
[2] And not 1885, as proposed in *Sherlock Holmes and Dr. Watson*, p. 28.
[3] Blakeney, op. cit., p. 63 ; see also p. 61.

Watson reports a remark which he says he made
to Holmes : ' Of the last six cases which I have
added to my notes, three have been entirely free
of any legal crime.' To this Holmes is repre-
sented as agreeing and naming the three other
cases cited above. According to Mr. Blakeney's
dating the last six cases before *The Blue Carbuncle*
are (reading backwards) *The Five Orange Pips*
(late September, 1889),[1] *The Engineer's Thumb*
(summer, 1889),[2] *The Crooked Man* (summer,
1889),[3] *The Naval Treaty* (July, 1889),[4] *The
Tired Captain* (July, 1889),[5] *The Man with the
Twisted Lip* (June, 1889).[6] Only one of
these, however, the last which we have listed,
is among those mentioned in the reply which
Watson attributes to Holmes, and in consequence the superstructure of conjecture con-
firmatory of the year 1888 as that of *The Sign
of Four* which Mr. Blakeney has built upon

[1] Op. cit., pp. 70 f.
[2] Ibid., pp. 59 f.
[3] Ibid., p. 60.
[4] Ibid., p. 69.
[5] Ibid., p. 70.
[6] Ibid., p. 61. The inclusion in the list of *The Second
Stain* (II), which Mr. Blakeney (pp. 38 f) seems to realise
must be a separate case from *The Second Stain* (III), and
which belongs in the same year and month as *The Naval
Treaty* and *The Tired Captain*, would not leave even one of
the three cases among the ' last six.'

the supposed correlation comes crashing to the ground.[1]

The passage under discussion is one which reveals Watson at his most 'editorial.' He seems sometimes to have felt at liberty to use matter from any period of his association with Holmes in the Introductory Discourse (which Father Knox calls the Prooimion) without much regard for historical accuracy. The classic example is his bodily transference of the Prooimion of *The Cardboard Box* to *The Resident Patient*.[2]

In the present state of our knowledge we must be resigned to the balancing of probabilities in attempting to date several of the tales. Among these, the most important for our present purpose is *The Five Orange Pips*. To Mr. Roberts[3] it is of crucial importance. He is prepared to ignore the great mass of opposing evidence in his desire to maintain the integrity of its reported date, and

[1] Our own schedule includes two of these three cases among the 'last six' before *The Blue Carbuncle*, and should therefore to that extent, at least, be more acceptable to Mr. Blakeney than his own.

[2] See *Sherlock Holmes and Dr. Watson*, pp. 40–45.

[3] *Dr. Watson*, pp. 17–18; in that work he dates *The Sign of Four* in 1886 without definitely suggesting a month, though apparently favouring some time between April and June (p. 16). In a more recent article in the *Observer* (October 30th, 1932) he seems to accept September.

is drawn logically to placing Watson's first marriage in June, 1887. Father Knox [1] accepts the date likewise ; but, in order to square it with his belief that the marriage occurred in 1888, rejects the reference to Mrs. Watson. He relies, unfortunately, upon the original text as published in the *Strand* and uncritically copied in some later editions, disregarding the revised text in the *Adventures* and in the *Complete Edition* (1928).

Mr. Blakeney's handling of *The Five Orange Pips* is even more original. He uses its irreconcilability with the 1887 dating of *The Sign of Four* and of Watson's first marriage as an argument against that year, and then proceeds to emend its date by two years in order to fit in into his own theory. Let him by all means emend it if he believes it wrong ; but he should not use that wrong date to discredit the date of another story. He cannot have it both ways.

The most valuable indications for determining the date of Watson's first marriage, and inferentially of *The Sign of Four*, are to be found in *The Noble Bachelor*. They are so elaborate and so entirely self-consistent that the arbitrary alteration of any one of them would destroy the possibility of dating the story on critical principles.

Let us examine them. On ' Oct. 4th ' Moulton

[1] Loc. cit.

paid his hotel bill,[1] communicated with his wife, and took her off to lodgings in Gordon Square. That day was, as we shall see, a Tuesday. Watson, in giving Holmes a *précis* of the affair, says: ' Two days later [2]—that is, on Wednesday last—there is a *curt announcement* [3] that the wedding had taken place '; and he goes on to say that ' a morning newspaper of yesterday ' mentions that ' the ceremony, as *shortly announced* [3] in the papers of yesterday,' occurred on the previous morning. From this it appears that Wednesday's ' curt announcement,' which must be the same as the short announcement, was published upon the day following the wedding, which therefore took place on the Tuesday. Since Moulton had paid

[1] Moulton took his wife to lodgings in Gordon Square in order to be quiet and to avoid the pursuit which they both must have known was inevitable. But he evidently kept his room at the hotel expecting to return there with her (she said that he was ' all for openness '). Having decided, however, at her persuasion to go on to Paris, he had to call at the hotel, pay for the room which he had retained and give it up, and perhaps collect some luggage. Hence Holmes when making his inquiries on Friday was told that he had left ' the day before.' This accords perfectly with the account given by Moulton and his wife.

[2] Referring back to a ' note in the *Morning Post* to say that the marriage would be an absolutely quiet one.' This note, two days before the ' curt announcement ' on Wednesday, appeared therefore on Monday.

[3] Italics ours.

his hotel bill up to the 4th,[1] the day of the wedding, October 4th, fell on a Tuesday. The day on which Holmes was consulted and on which he solved the problem was therefore a Friday.[2]

Watson, at the beginning of his narrative, tells us that the adventure befell 'a few weeks before' his own marriage.[3] Two different years have been proposed as the date of that event, 1887,[4] and 1888.[5] In 1887 October 4th was a Tuesday. We cannot alter 'Wednesday' to 'Friday' in order to conform to Mr. Blakeney's dating, since the change would give us Sunday as the day of Lord Robert St. Simon's visit to Holmes [6]—the day, that is, on which Holmes ordered in a cold

---

[1] He had it with him in the church.

[2] And not Thursday, as stated in *Sherlock Holmes and Dr. Watson*, p. 38.

[3] It should be observed that he is still suffering from his injured heel, which may have been further strained by his 'six-mile limp' nine days before. To a newly-engaged man the situation must have been most irksome.

[4] S. C. Roberts: *Dr. Watson*, pp. 16–18; Desmond MacCarthy, in *The Listener* for December 11th, 1929; H. W. Bell: *Sherlock Holmes and Dr. Watson*, pp. 49–55.

[5] R. A. Knox: *Essays in Satire*, p. 155; also in *New Statesman* for November 12th, 1932; T. S. Blakeney, *Sherlock Holmes; Fact or Fiction?* pp. 54–64.

[6] In 1888, October 9th fell on Tuesday, but in view of the results of Miss Dorothy L. Sayers' study of Watson's handwriting, we cannot alter '4' to '9.'

supper from the confectioner's, and on which he received a delivery of letters.[1]

We must also remember that Watson refers to *The Noble Bachelor* as ' this four-year-old drama.' Since his account was first published in April, 1892, it could hardly have been written later than February, or four years and four months at the very furthest after the events described if, as we believe, they took place in October, 1887. On Mr. Blakeney's theory the interval would be reduced to a few months over three years.

[1] ' Your morning letters, if I remember right, were from a fishmonger and a tide-waiter.'

NOTE ON DR. WATSON'S WOUND

THE disablement which Watson received at the battle of Maiwand (July 27th, 1880) has puzzled some commentators and led them to imply that he himself was uncertain whether it was in his shoulder or in his foot.[1] Such uncertainty on his part, if it indeed existed, would be inexplicable, and would cast grave doubts upon his general trustworthiness. It is therefore necessary to examine the data and see what conclusions arise from them.

1881. Watson tells us that he was 'struck on the shoulder by a Jezail bullet, which shattered the bone and grazed the subclavian artery.'[2] While recovering in the hospital at Peshawur he was 'struck down by enteric fever,' his life was despaired of, and he became so weak and emaciated that when at length convalescent he was sent back to England. There he arrived with shaken nerves, unable to stand much noise or excitement, and

[1] E.g., Desmond MacCarthy: 'Dr. Watson' (*The Listener*, December 11th, 1929), p. 776.

[2] *A Study in Scarlet*, II, 5. From a remark of Holmes' (II, 22) we learn that the injury was to the left shoulder.

with his health, as he thought, irretrievably ruined.[1] His appearance, according to Holmes, was haggard, and his condition such that he could not venture out unless the weather were exceptionally genial.[2] The exertion and excitements of the morning of March 4th, 1881, overtaxed his precarious strength, and he was obliged in consequence to spend the afternoon on the sofa.[3] It is worthy of note, in view of his later exploits, that he took no part in restraining Jefferson Hope from throwing himself out of the window.[4]

1887. 'I . . . sat nursing my wounded leg. I had had a Jezail bullet through it some time before, and, though it did not prevent me from walking, it ached wearily at every change in the weather.'[5]

'I limped impatiently about the room.'[6]

'I, an Army Surgeon with a weak leg.'[7]

Holmes inquires :

'Are you game for a six-mile trudge, Watson ?'

'Certainly,' I answered.

'Your leg will stand it ?'[8]

Later in the same chapter Holmes refers to their expedition with Toby as 'a six-mile limp for a half-pay officer with a damaged tendo Achillis.'[9] Some days later the rainy weather made his wound ache and incapacitated him for at least one day.[10]

1890. Holmes, in explaining his thought-reading

---

[1] II, 6.
[2] II, 15.
[3] II, 44–45.
[4] II, 72.
[5] *The Sign of Four*, II, 146.
[6] Ibid., 150.
[7] Ibid., 158.
[8] Ibid., 198.
[9] Ibid., 202.
[10] *The Noble Bachelor*, I, 224–225.

process to Watson, tells him : ' Your hand stole towards your own old wound.' [1]

1897. Watson mentions his wound-pension.[2]

With the foregoing data the following should be compared.

1882. ' We had been walking briskly.' [3]

1884. The run of two miles without halting.[4]

1886. ' We were both fair runners and in good condition.' [5]

' Blindly we ran through the gloom.' [6]

' Never have I seen a man run as Holmes did that night. I am reckoned fleet of foot, but he outpaced me.' [7]

1887. ' I rushed madly from the room on to the landing.' [8]

1889. ' In a quarter of an hour [after leaving Baker Street] we were in Bloomsbury at the Alpha Inn.' [9]

1890. ' He dashed up, the Inspector and I at his heels.' [10]

1891. ' The instant your cab stops, dash through the Arcade.'

[1] *The Cardboard Box*, I, 926.

[2] *Shoscombe Old Place*, I, 1301.

[3] *Silver Blaze*, I, 321.

[4] *Charles Augustus Milverton*, I, 737.

[5] *The Hound of the Baskervilles*, II, 377.

[6] Ibid., 411.

[7] Ibid., 435.

[8] *The Reigate Squires*, I, 431.

[9] *The Blue Carbuncle*, I, 162. Since the distance covered was about one mile and five-eighths, the rate was a mile in less than $9\frac{1}{2}$ minutes.

[10] *The Greek Interpreter*, I, 495.

' I drove . . . to the Lowther Arcade, through which
I hurried at the top of my speed.' [1]

1895. ' We ran frantically down the path.' [2]

These passages are ample proof that Watson
was wounded both in the heel [3] and in the left
shoulder; and it is evident that the inaccuracy,
or worse, with which, in this connection, he has
been charged, is due to his native reticence.
Human nature being what it is, such modesty is
always in danger of misinterpretation. It is
pleasant to observe that, in spite of the de-
spondency and pessimism in which he was
plunged at the time of his introduction to
Holmes, his recovery, though slow, seems to
have been complete. [4]

[1] *The Final Problem*, I, 545, 546. There is also the
walking-tour up the Rhône Valley and over the Gemmi to
Meiringen, *via* Interlaken.

[2] *The Solitary Cyclist*, I, 654.

[3] See Miss Helen Simpson's article (above, p. 45, note 1)
for a most interesting and plausible suggestion regarding
the origin of this wound.

[4] By 1895 his sensitiveness to cold and damp had
vanished. He walked four miles at night in the rain
(*Wisteria Lodge*, I, 904-5).